Born in Buncrana, Co. Donegal, Frank McGuinness now lives in Dublin and lectures in English at St Patrick's College, Maynooth. He has also worked at the University of Ulster, Coleraine, and at University College, Dublin.

For the Abbey Theatre he has written *The Factory Girls*, *Baglady*, and in 1985 the celebrated *Observe the Sons of Ulster Marching Towards the Somme* which won many awards, including the London *Evening Standard* Most Promising Playwright Award, an Arts Council Bursary, the 1987 Ewart-Biggs Peace Prize, the 1985 Harvey's Best Play Award and the Cheltenham Literary Prize. His play *Innocence* (on the life of Caravaggio) premièred at the Gate Theatre in October 1986. His new version of Lorca's *Yerma* was produced at the Abbey Theatre in May 1987 and a new version of Ibsen's *Rosmersholm*, commissioned by the National Theatre of Great Britain, opened in the same week. *Carthaginians* received its première during the 1988 Dublin Theatre Festival, and was also produced at the Hampstead Theatre. In 1988 the Gate Theatre produced his version of *Peer Gynt*. His play *Mary and Lizzie* was performed at the Barbican in 1989.

THREE SISTERS

by ANTON CHEKHOV

a version by
Frank McGuinness

from a literal translation
by Rose Cullen

faber and faber
LONDON · BOSTON

For Peter and Siobhan Denman

First published in 1990
by Faber and Faber Limited
3 Queen Square London WC1N 3AU

Photoset by Parker Typesetting Service Leicester
Printed in England by Clays Ltd St Ives plc

© Frank McGuinness, 1990

A CIP record for this book is available from
the British Library.

ISBN 0-571-16171-5

This version of *Three Sisters* was first performed at the Gate Theatre, Dublin in March 1990. The cast was as follows:

OLGA ⎫	Sorcha Cusack
IRINA ⎬ three sisters	Niamh Cusack
MASHA ⎭	Sinead Cusack
CHEBUTYKIN, IVAN ROMANOVICH, army doctor	Cyril Cusack
TUZENBACH, NIKOLAI L'VOVICH, baron, lieutenant	Barry Lynch
SOLENYI, VASILII VASIL'EVICH, staff captain	Sean McGinley
FERAPONT SPIRIDONYCH, watchman	Seamus Forde
ANFISA, nanny	Anna Manahan
VERSHININ, ALEKSANDR IGNAT'EVICH, lieutenant-colonel, battery-commander	Michael Pennington
ANDREI SERGEEVICH PROZOROV, brother to Olga, Irina and Masha	Mark Lambert
KULYGIN, FEDOR IL'ICH, Masha's husband	Tom Hickey
NATASHA, NATALIA IVANOVNA Andrei's fiancée, later his wife	Orla Brady
FEDOTIK, ALEKSEI PETROVICH, second lieutenant	Mark O'Regan
RODE, VLADIMIR KARLOVICH, second lieutenant	Jonathan Sharpe
SOLDIER	John Bergin
MAIDS	Karen Ardiff
	Geraldine Judge
BOBIK	Aidan Hanratty
Director	Adrian Noble
Designer	Bob Crowley
Lighting Designer	Rupert Murray

ACT ONE

The Prozorov house.
*There is a drawing room with columns, behind which a large
ballroom can be seen. Outside, the weather is sunny and bright. In
the ballroom, the table is being set for lunch.*

   OLGA, *wearing the blue uniform dress of a girls' secondary school
teacher, stands up and moves about. She constantly corrects her
pupils' exercise books.* MASHA *wears a black dress, sitting with her
hat on her lap, reading a book. In a white dress,* IRINA *stands lost
in thought.*

OLGA: Father died a year ago. This day exactly. Your saint's
       day, Irina. Fifth of May. It was bitterly cold, then; it was
       snowing. I thought I'd never endure it. You fainted. Lying
       there as if you were dead. But now a year's gone, and we
       can talk about it easily. There you are, wearing white – and
       your face is open to the world.
       (*The clock strikes twelve.*)
       The clock chimed then as well.
       (*Pause.*)
       I remember music playing when they shouldered Father,
       and they fired a salute at the graveyard. He was a general,
       he commanded a brigade. But there were few enough
       people there. Naturally, it was raining at the time. Raining
       and snowing hard.
IRINA: Why talk about it?
       (BARON TUZENBACH, CHEBUTYKIN *and* SOLENYI *appear
       from behind the ballroom columns, close to the table.*)
OLGA: Isn't it warm today? We can leave the windows wide
       open, the birch trees aren't even in leaf. Eleven years ago
       Father was given his brigade, and we left Moscow. I
       distinctly remember Moscow at this time of year, the
       beginning of May. Everything blossomed; it was warm, all
       washed by the sun. Eleven years ago, yet I remember
       everything. It's as if we left yesterday. God, I woke up this

I

morning, and I saw this light, it's spring, and my heart danced, I was so happy. I so much wanted to be back home.

CHEBUTYKIN: The devil it is.

TUZENBACH: Rubbish, yes, of course.

(*Brooding on a book*, MASHA *whistles a song.*)

OLGA: Masha, do not whistle, it's not right.

(*Pause.*)

I'm in school all day, then I give lessons until the evening, my head is always splitting and I'm thinking like an old woman already. Honest to God, the four years I've worked in that school, they've drained my strength and my youth. Drop by drop, every day. And one dream gets more and more real.

IRINA: Leave for Moscow. Sell the house, settle everything here, and – leave for Moscow.

OLGA: Yes! Moscow, go there as soon as we can.

(CHEBUTYKIN *and* TUZENBACH *laugh.*)

IRINA: Andrei will probably become a professor. One thing's sure, he won't stay here. Poor Masha, that's the only problem.

OLGA: Masha will come to Moscow for the entire summer every year.

(MASHA *softly whistles a song.*)

IRINA: God willing, everything will be all right.

(*She looks through the window.*)

Isn't the weather beautiful today? Why is my heart so light? This morning I remembered it was my feast day and suddenly I was happy. I could remember when I was small, Mama was still alive. Such wonderful times, such wonderful memories. I was thrilled. The thought of it.

OLGA: The sun shines on you today. You look so strange, so beautiful. And Masha is beautiful this morning. Andrei would be a fine-looking man but he puts on so much weight, and it doesn't suit him. And you can be sure I've aged and turned to skin and bone because I get cross with the girls at school. But today, I've no teaching and my head isn't splitting, so I feel younger than yesterday. I'm only twenty-eight . . . Everything's all right, it's God's will, but I think I

2

should have married and stayed in the house all the time, because things would have been better.

(*Pause.*)

I would have loved my husband.

(TUZENBACH *speaks to* SOLENYI.)

TUZENBACH: You talk absolute rubbish, I'm tired listening to you. (*Enters the drawing room.*) I forgot to tell you. Today our new Battery Commander will call on you. Vershinin. (*Sits at the piano.*)

OLGA: Well, that's good.

IRINA: Is he old?

TUZENBACH: No, not exactly. Forty, forty-five, thereabouts. (*Plays quietly.*) A nice fellow, I think. Not stupid, that's certain. He does talk. A lot.

IRINA: Is he attractive?

TUZENBACH: Yes, he's all right, but he has a wife, a mother-in-law, and two little girls. Second wife, what's more. Wherever he goes, he talks about his wife and two little girls. He'll bore you with them as well. The wife's a bit touched. A long plait in her hair like a girl's. She takes flight when she talks, calls it philosophy, and is addicted to suicide. This is intended to disturb her husband. A woman like that I would have left ages ago, but he takes it all on and offers it up. He just keeps complaining about it.

(SOLENYI *enters the drawing room with* CHEBUTYKIN. CHEBUTYKIN *reads the newspaper on his way in.*)

SOLENYI: With one hand, I can lift only fifty pounds. Two hands, I can lift a hundred and eighty, even two hundred pounds. From this I deduce that two people are not twice as strong as one, but three times stronger, perhaps even more.

CHEBUTYKIN: For baldness: Two measures of naphthalene to half a bottle of methylated spirit . . . dissolve, apply daily. (*Writes in a little notebook.*) Write that down. (*Addresses* SOLENYI) Now, I was saying, a cork is placed in the bottle, a little glass tube is passed through it . . . Then, take a pinch of simple, ordinary arum.

IRINA: Ivan Romanych, dear Ivan Romanych!

CHEBUTYKIN: What is it, my good girl?

3

IRINA: Tell me, what's making me so happy this day? I feel I'm on a ship, there's a great, blue sky above me and white, white birds float all around me. What is it? What?

(CHEBUTYKIN *tenderly kisses her two hands*.)

CHEBUTYKIN: My white bird . . .

IRINA: I woke up this morning, and while I was getting up and washing, everything on this earth suddenly seemed to be so clear to me. I knew how life must be lived. Dear Ivan Romanych, I know all things. Man must work, no matter who he is, work by the sweat of his brow. There lies the meaning of his life. His purpose, his happiness, his joy. It is good to be a worker, rising at dawn, breaking stones on the roadside, or a shepherd, or a teacher who instructs the young, or an engine driver on the railway: one doesn't need to be human to work. The simple beasts of the field work, better to be them than a young woman who rises at twelve, drinks coffee in bed and then spends two hours dressing. How terrible. I long for work as one longs for a drink in hot weather . . . If I don't start getting up early and working, then refuse to be my friend, Ivan Romanych.

(CHEBUTYKIN *speaks to her tenderly*.)

CHEBUTYKIN: I will refuse, I will.

OLGA: Father raised us to get up at seven o'clock. Now Irina wakes at seven and lies in bed until at least nine o'clock, thinking about something or other. And she has such a serious look on her face. (*Laughs*.)

IRINA: You only see me as a child, you're surprised when I have a serious look on my face. I'm twenty years old.

TUZENBACH: The desire to work, God, I understand that so well. I've never done a day's work. Frozen, frigid Petersburg, that's where I was born. My family didn't know the meaning of work or worry. I would come home from cadet school, I remember some lackey would pull off my boots. I'd behave badly, and my mother would look and admire me. She was shocked when others saw me in a different light. I was protected from work. But I doubt if they'll succeed totally. I doubt that. The time has come. A great cloud of thunder approaches us all. A fierce, cleansing storm is on its way. It's

4

already very near and it will purge our society, the idleness, the indifference, the reluctance to work and the rotting boredom. I will work, and everyone will work within twenty-five, thirty years. Everyone.

CHEBUTYKIN: I won't work.

TUZENBACH: You don't count.

SOLENYI: In twenty-five years, thank God, you won't be here. In two or three years you'll have a stroke and die, or else I'll lose my temper and fire a bullet into your brain, my angel.

(SOLENYI *takes a flask of scent from his pocket and sprinkles his hands and chest.* CHEBUTYKIN *laughs.*)

CHEBUTYKIN: To tell the truth, I've never done anything at all. Since leaving university I've never lifted a finger. I haven't read one book, only newspapers. (*Takes out another newspaper from his pocket.*) Look here . . . I know from the paper such a person as Dobroliubov existed, but what did he actually write about? I don't know . . . God knows . . .

(*Knocking is heard from the floor below.*)

Now . . . downstairs, they're calling me . . . someone's come for me . . . I'll be back in a moment . . . one moment. (*Makes a hurried exit, combing his beard.*)

IRINA: Something is afoot.

TUZENBACH: Yes. The solemn look on exit. He is obviously bringing you a present.

IRINA: Oh no, no.

OLGA: Oh yes. It's dreadful. He is always doing something silly.

(MASHA *stands up and hums softly.*)

MASHA: I saw the shore that strides the sea,
    A green, green oak, oh green oak tree,
    A chain of gold embracing thee,
    A chain of gold embracing thee.
    A wise green cat beneath that tree . . .

OLGA: You're not happy today, Masha.

(MASHA *continues humming, putting on her hat.*)

Where are you going?

MASHA: Home.

IRINA: That's strange . . .

TUZENBACH: Leaving a feast-day party!

MASHA: What difference? I'll be back this evening. Goodbye, loved one. (*Kisses* IRINA.) Again I wish you health and happiness. When Father was alive, in the old days, thirty or forty officers would come every feast day – there was life. Today there are one and a half men present and correct. It's dead, dead – I'm leaving . . . I'm depressed today. Sad. Pay me no attention. (*Laughs through tears.*) Later, we'll talk, but now, goodbye, my love. I'll wander somewhere or other.

(IRINA *is displeased.*)

IRINA: You are absolutely –

(OLGA *speaks through tears.*)

OLGA: I understand you, Masha.

SOLENYI: A man talks philosophy, it *is* philosophy, or at least sophistry. A woman, or two women, talk philosophy, and end up tearing out their hair.

MASHA: What does that mean, you awful man?

SOLENYI: Nothing. The bear, the bear, beware the bear, it laid him low, no, oh no.

(*Silence.*

MASHA *speaks angrily to* OLGA.)

MASHA: Stop bawling.

(ANFISA *and* FERAPONT *enter with a cake.*)

ANFISA: This way, my dear, come in. Your feet are clean. (*To* IRINA) From Mikhail Ivanych Protopopov at the council . . . a cake.

IRINA: Thank you. Tell him, thank you.

FERAPONT: What?

IRINA: (*Raises her voice*) Thank you, tell him.

OLGA: Nanny, give him a piece of cake. Go along, Ferapont, they'll give you a piece of cake.

ANFISA: Come along, dear Ferapont Spindonyon, come along. (*Leaves with* FERAPONT.)

MASHA: I dislike that Protopopov. Mikhail or Ivanych, whatever his name is. He shouldn't be invited.

IRINA: I didn't.

MASHA: Good . . .

(CHEBUTYKIN *enters. A soldier, behind him, carries a silver*

6

samovar. There is a hum of astonishment and displeasure. OLGA *covers her face with her hands.*)

OLGA: A samovar. A solid silver samovar. Dreadful, dreadful.
(*She goes to the table in the ballroom.* IRINA, TUZENBACH *and* MASHA *speak together.*)

IRINA: My dear Romanych, what are you up to?

TUZENBACH: I told you, I told you.

MASHA: Ivan Romanych, you should be ashamed of yourself.

CHEBUTYKIN: Dear good girls, you are all I have. In this whole world, you are most precious to me. Sixty years old I am soon. An old man. Lonely, worthless. An old man . . . There is nothing good in me, but I love you, and I would have left this world long ago if it had not been for you.
(*To* IRINA) Dear child, I've known you since the hour you were born . . . I nursed you in my arms . . . I loved your dead mother . . .

IRINA: But these expensive presents, why –
(CHEBUTYKIN *speaks angrily through tears.*)

CHEBUTYKIN: Expensive presents. Get away with you.
(*Addresses the soldier*) Put the samovar over there.
(*Mocking* IRINA) These expensive presents.
(*The soldier takes the samovar into the ballroom.* ANFISA *crosses the drawing room.*)

ANFISA: A strange colonel is here, my loves. He's taken off his coat already, children. He is on his way in here. Irinushka, see to it that you are friendly and well-mannered to him.
(*Goes out, remarking*) It's well past lunchtime. Heavens . . .

TUZENBACH: It must be Vershinin.
(VERSHININ *enters.*)
Lieutenant-Colonel Vershinin.
(VERSHININ *addresses* MASHA *and* IRINA.)

VERSHININ: May I introduce myself? Vershinin. You've changed so much. My, my.

IRINA: Sit down please. We're delighted to see you.
(VERSHININ *is cheerful.*)

VERSHININ: I am so pleased. So pleased. Weren't there three sisters? Three little girls, I remember. I can't recognize your faces, but I distinctly remember that your father, Colonel

Prozorov, had three little girls. I saw them with my own eyes. Time flies. My, my, time flies.

TUZENBACH: Aleksandr Ignatevich has come from Moscow.

IRINA: Moscow? You're from Moscow?

VERSHININ: Yes. Your late father was a battery commander there and I was an officer in the same brigade. (*Turns to* MASHA) I have a vague memory of your face.

MASHA: I have no memory of you.

IRINA: Olia, Olia?

(*Calls into the ballroom*) Come here, Olia.

(OLGA *enters from the ballroom.*)

IRINA: It seems that Lieutenant-Colonel Vershinin comes from Moscow.

VERSHININ: You must be Olga Sergeevna, the oldest – and you are Maria . . . And you, the youngest, Irina.

OLGA: You are from Moscow?

VERSHININ: Yes. I studied in Moscow. That's where I began my service and I was stationed there for a long time. I was eventually given command of the battery in this place and so, as you can see, I've moved here. I can't remember you clearly, just the fact that there were three of you. Your father's face, that memory's strong. I close my eyes, I can see him as if he were still living. I used to visit you in Moscow . . .

OLGA: I thought I could remember everyone, yet suddenly –

VERSHININ: My name is Aleksandr Ignatevich.

IRINA: Aleksandr Ignatevich, who is from Moscow. What a surprise.

OLGA: We're moving there, you see.

IRINA: Come autumn, we think we'll be there. It's our home, our place of birth . . . in Staryi Basmannyi Street.

(IRINA *and* OLGA *laugh joyously.*)

MASHA: I remember now. Olia, you remember, all the talk about the Lovesick Major. Weren't you a lieutenant then? You were in love with someone, and everyone would tease you, calling you the Major for some reason.

(VERSHININ *laughs.*)

VERSHININ: Quite right, yes . . . Lovesick Major . . . that's right.

MASHA: You only had a moustache then. You look so much older. (*Speaks through tears*) Older, so much older.

VERSHININ: The Lovesick Major was young and in love. He is neither now.

OLGA: There isn't a single grey hair on your head. You've aged, but you're not an old man yet.

VERSHININ: Well, next birthday, I'm forty-three years old. Have you been away from Moscow for long?

IRINA: Eleven years. Masha, you silly girl, why are you crying now? I'll cry as well –

MASHA: I'm fine. What street did you live on?

VERSHININ: Staryi Basmannyi.

OLGA: Our street.

VERSHININ: One time I lived in Nemetskii Street. I used to walk from Nemetskii to the Krasnyi Barracks. There's a dark bridge on the way there, water rushing beneath it. A bad place for a lonely man.
(*Silence.*)
The river here is so wide and flowing. A wonderful river.

OLGA: But it's cold. So cold here. There are mosquitoes.

VERSHININ: Really? The climate is so fine here, healthy, Russian . . . Forest, river and the birch trees, the good, humble birch trees. I love them above all other trees. This is a good place to live. The only odd thing is that the railway station is fifteen miles away, and no one knows why.

SOLENYI: I know why.
(*They all look at him.*)
If it were any nearer then it wouldn't be further, and if it were any further, then it wouldn't be nearer.
(*There is an uncomfortable silence.*)

TUZENBACH: A bit of a comedian, this man.

OLGA: Now, I remember you. Yes, I remember.

VERSHININ: I knew your mother.

CHEBUTYKIN: A good woman, God rest her soul.

IRINA: Mama is buried in Moscow.

OLGA: In Novodevichi.

MASHA: I've begun to forget her face already. Would you believe

I could forget? The same way we'll be forgotten. We'll be forgotten.

VERSHININ: Yes. We will be forgotten. That's our fate. There's nothing you can do. A time will come when what seems so serious, so significant, so profound to us will be forgotten or will be dismissed entirely.

(*Silence.*)

Isn't it fascinating that we have no exact way of knowing what will be considered elevated and profound, and what will be laughed at and pitied? Take the discoveries of Copernicus, or Columbus. Weren't they deemed ridiculous at first? Worthless? But some old nonsense scribbled by a crank, *that* was believed to be true. So it may be with the way we lead our lives. We accept it without questioning it, but will it seem strange, perverse, foolish, without principle, even, possibly, sinful?

TUZENBACH: Who knows? Maybe our way of life will be honoured as a great age. Maybe it will be remembered with respect. These days we don't have torture, executions or invasions, but there is suffering, so much of it, too.

SOLENYI: (*Adopts a reedy voice*) Cheep-cheep-cheep. Get the Baron on his philosophy and forget everything else.

TUZENBACH: Vasilii Vasil'ich, be a good man and leave me be. (*Sits in a different place.*) It is rather boring.

SOLENYI: Cheep-cheep-cheep.

(TUZENBACH *speaks to* VERSHININ.)

TUZENBACH: When you see suffering today – and there is so much, so much of it – you do realize, however, that in certain ways society has improved itself –

VERSHININ: Yes, of course, yes.

CHEBUTYKIN: Baron, you've just said our age will be honoured as a great one, but people are small. (*Stands up.*) Look at how small I am. You only say my life is great so you can console me . . .

(*A violin plays.*)

MASHA: That's Andrei playing – our brother.

IRINA: The family scholar. He'll become a professor probably. Papa was a soldier, but his son chose an academic career for himself.

MASHA: Papa wanted that.

OLGA: We've been teasing him today. We think he is a little bit in love.

IRINA: With one of the local young ladies. She's sure to visit us today.

MASHA: Oh God, the way that woman dresses. I don't mind her having neither taste nor style, but it's absolutely pathetic. I mean, that extraordinary skirt, lurid, some sort of yellow; the fringe, it's so vulgar. And a red blouse. Her cheeks look like they've been scrubbed by brushes. Andrei is not in love, I won't believe that. He does have some taste, he must have. He is doing this to tease us. He's acting the idiot. I learned yesterday she's to marry Protopopov, the president of the local council. A perfect match. (*Calls through the side door*) Andrei, come here. For a moment, love.

(ANDREI *enters.*)

OLGA: My brother, Andrei Sergeich.

VERSHININ: Vershinin.

ANDREI: Prozorov. (*Wipes his sweating face.*)
You're the new battery commander?

OLGA: Listen, Aleksandr Ignatevich is from Moscow.

ANDREI: Really? Congratulations – now my sisters will give you no peace.

VERSHININ: I've already managed to tire your sisters out.

IRINA: Look, this little picture frame, Andrei gave it to me today. (*Shows the frame.*) He made it himself.
(*At a loss for words,* VERSHININ *looks at the frame.*)

VERSHININ: Really . . . very nice, very . . .

IRINA: That little frame, above the piano, he made it too.
(*Waving his hand dismissively,* ANDREI *goes off.*)

OLGA: He's the scholar amongst us, and he plays the violin, and he makes all kinds of things. Honestly, he can turn his hand to anything. Andrei, don't go. This habit of his – always running away. Come here.
(*Taking him by the arms,* MASHA *and* IRINA *laughingly lead him back.*)

MASHA: Come on, come on.

ANDREI: Let me be, please.

MASHA: You're so silly. Aleksandr Ignatevich was christened the Lovesick Major. Did he get cross? Not in the slightest.

VERSHININ: Not in the slightest.

MASHA: I'm going to call you the Lovesick Fiddler.

IRINA: Or the Lovesick Professor.

OLGA: He's in love, little Andrei's in love.

(IRINA *applauds*.)

IRINA: Yes, yes, more, Andrei is in love.

(CHEBUTYKIN *comes up behind* ANDREI *and embraces him around the waist*.)

CHEBUTYKIN: Nature loves us, so she creates us, why? To love and love. (*Guffaws, the newspaper still in his hand*.)

ANDREI: Enough, enough, all right. (*Wipes his face*.) I didn't close my eyes last night, now I'm not quite all there, as they say. I read until four, then got into bed, but nothing happened. I thought about this and that, but dawn breaks early here, the light pours into my bedroom. Since we'll be here for the summer, there's a particular book I'd like to translate from English.

VERSHININ: You can read English?

ANDREI: Yes. Father, God rest him, crammed us with knowledge. This will sound totally ridiculous, but I've still got to confess it. Since he died I've piled on weight and within one year I've got fat. It's as if my body's broken free. Thanks to Father we all know French, German and English. Irina knows Italian as well. But it's all taken its toll.

MASHA: In this town knowing three languages is a useless luxury. No, not a luxury, more of a freak, a hand with six fingers. We know a lot that is useless.

VERSHININ: Come now! (*Laughs*.) You know a lot that is useless? Does such a town exist, so dull, so dismal that an intelligent, educated person has no use being there? I put it to you. There are one hundred thousand people in this town, primitive and coarse as they unquestionably are, and then there are three such as you. Only three, surrounded by a flood of ignorance. Reason tells you that you can't succeed against that. As you lead your life, you'll give in, day by day, and you'll be lost in that crowd one hundred thousand strong. Life will defeat you, and yet will you vanish without trace? After you, maybe six more like you will suddenly appear, and then twelve more, and so on until you form the majority. Give this earthly life two, three hundred more years. It will be beautiful beyond belief, beyond imagination. Man must foresee it, wait for it, dream of it, prepare for it. To succeed, we must have greater experience, greater knowledge than our ancestors possessed. (*Laughs*.) And yet you complain. You know a lot that is useless?

(MASHA *takes off her hat*.)

MASHA: I'm staying for lunch.

(IRINA *sighs*.)

IRINA: Oh why didn't someone write all of that down?

(ANDREI *is not there. He has slipped out unnoticed*.)

TUZENBACH: So far away in the future, you say, life will be beautiful beyond belief. Point taken. But to shape it in the here and now, with only a distant view, one must prepare one's self for it, work, we must –

VERSHININ: Yes. (*Gets up*.) You have flowers everywhere. (*Glances around*.) What gorgeous rooms. I'm jealous of you. Flats with two chairs, a sofa, a stove forever smoking, that's where I've hung about all my life. My life's lacked these flowers. (*Rubs his hands*.) So. Never mind.

TUZENBACH: Yes, one must work. I know, I know what you're thinking. Listen to the sentimental German. But I give you my word, I'm Russian. Can't even speak German. My father belonged to the Orthodox faith.

(*Silence.*

VERSHININ *walks about the stage*.)

VERSHININ: I wonder, I wonder, what would happen if you were to start life afresh, but this time, know everything? The first life, the one already lived, there's the rough draft. The other life, the new one, that's the fair copy. Were that possible, I would say above all else each of us would try not to repeat himself. At least lead a different kind of life. Find rooms such as these, full of flowers, full of light. I have a wife, two little girls, and what's more, my wife's not well, and so on and so on. Well, were I to start my life afresh, I wouldn't get married. No, no.

(KULYGIN *enters, wearing a teacher's uniform. He goes up to* IRINA.)

KULYGIN: Dear sister, may I be permitted to congratulate you on your saint's feast day, and may I, with sincerity, with deep affection, may I wish you health and all that a girl your age could desire? May I be permitted to present you with this little book? A gift. (*Gives her the book.*) The history of our school, its whole fifty years. I wrote it. A minor little book, written when I had nothing better to do, but do read it even so. Good day ladies and gentlemen. (*Addresses* VERSHININ.) Kulygin, teacher, local secondary school, court counsellor. (*Addresses* IRINA.) In this book you will find listed all those who have completed their studies in our school over those fifty years. *Feci quod potui, facient meliore potentes . . .* (*Kisses* MASHA.)

IRINA: You gave me this book already, last Easter.

(KULYGIN *laughs.*)

KULYGIN: No? Impossible! Then give it back to me. Better still, give it to the Colonel. Take it, Colonel, please. Do read it some time, when you've nothing better to do.

VERSHININ: Thank you.

(*Gets ready to leave.*) I'm very glad to have made your acquaintance.

OLGA: Don't leave, please.

IRINA: Stay and lunch with us, please.

OLGA: Please do.

(VERSHININ *bows.*)

VERSHININ: It seems I've barged into a feast-day party. Forgive me, I didn't know and haven't congratulated you.

(*He goes into the ballroom with* OLGA.)

KULYGIN: Ladies and gentlemen, this day is the Sabbath, a day of rest. Therefore let us rest, let us amuse ourselves as befits our age and our situation. Those carpets should be taken up for the summer and locked away till winter . . . Use some Persian powder or naphthalene . . . Rome bred a healthy people because they knew how to work and how to play.

Mens sana in corpore sano, that's what formed them. That's what shaped them, that's what established them. Our headmaster says, in any way of life, nothing is more important than its form . . . whatever loses form is finished – and the same goes for the way we lead our everyday lives. (*Puts his arm around* MASHA's *waist, laughing.*) Masha loves me. My wife loves me. The curtains should go with the carpets . . . I'm happy today, excellent mental shape. Masha, at four o'clock today, the headmaster's expecting us at his house. An outing has been arranged for the teachers and their families.

MASHA: I'm not going.

(KULYGIN *is aggrieved.*)

KULYGIN: Why not, dear Masha?

MASHA: Later, we'll talk about it later . . . All right, I'll go . . . just, please leave me alone.

(*She walks away.*)

KULYGIN: And then we'll spend the evening at the headmaster's house. Constantly ill, and yet that man does not cease to be sociable. A noble individual, outstanding. After the meeting, yesterday, he said to me, I'm tired, Fedor Il'ich, I'm tired. (*He looks at the clock on the wall, then checks his watch.*) Seven minutes fast, your clock. Yes, he said, I'm tired. (*Offstage the violin plays.*)

OLGA: Gentlemen, please, lunch. We have a pie.

KULYGIN: Ah, Olga, my dearest. I worked yesterday from break of day until eleven at night. So tired, but today I'm happy. (*Goes to the table in the ballroom.*) My dearest . . .

(CHEBUTYKIN *puts the newspaper in his pocket and combs his hair.*)

CHEBUTYKIN: Pie. Excellent.

(MASHA *speaks sternly to* CHEBUTYKIN.)

MASHA: Now, you, watch it. Not one drop today, do you hear me? Drink is bad for you.

CHEBUTYKIN: What's wrong with you? That's in the past. It's been two years since I did any heavy drinking. (*Grows impatient.*) So what, my dear? What does it matter?

MASHA: Even so, do not dare touch a drop of drink.

(*She speaks angrily but out of her husband's earshot.*)
Damnation. An eternal evening being bored, in the house of the headmaster. Again.

TUZENBACH: I wouldn't go if I were you . . . it's very simple.

CHEBUTYKIN: Don't go, loved one.

MASHA: Don't go, oh yes . . . This damned life, I cannot endure it.
(*She goes to the ballroom.*
CHEBUTYKIN *goes to her.*)

CHEBUTYKIN: There, there.
(SOLENYI *crosses to the ballroom.*)

SOLENYI: Cheep-cheep-cheep.
(KULYGIN *is cheerful.*)

KULYGIN: Good health, Colonel. I'm a teacher, one of the family, this is home, Masha's husband . . . She's kind, very kind.

VERSHININ: I'll take some of this dark vodka. (*Drinks.*) Good health.
(*Addresses* OLGA.) It is so good to be here.
(*Only* IRINA *and* TUZENBACH *remain in the drawing room.*)

IRINA: Masha is not well today. She married when she was eighteen. Then she thought him the cleverest of men. Not so. The kindest of men, not the cleverest.
(OLGA *is impatient.*)

OLGA: Andrei, hurry up.

ANDREI: (*Off*) Coming.
(*He enters and goes to the table.*)

TUZENBACH: A penny for your thoughts?

IRINA: Your Solenyi, I don't like him. He talks rubbish all the time.

TUZENBACH: A strange man, yes. I pity him, he annoys me as well, but I pity him more. He's shy, I think . . . when we're together, the two of us, he's very clever, a friend, but let him loose in company, he's a boor, a bully. Don't go. Let them arrange themselves at table. Let me be close to you, just for a moment. A penny for your thoughts?
(*Silence.*)
You're twenty years old, and I'm not thirty yet. Years stretch in front of us, how many years? Days and days in their long

16

line, my love for you, in every long –

IRINA: Nikolai L'vovich, don't mention love to me.

(TUZENBACH *does not listen.*)

TUZENBACH: You see, I want to drink passionately from life, struggle, work, I am dry, and I am so because I am – my heart – is in love with you, Irina. Because *you* are beautiful, life is full of beauty to me as well. A penny for your thoughts.

IRINA: You say, life is full of beauty, so it appears to you. We are three sisters, for us, life has not been full of beauty . . . Choking us, like weeds choke flowers . . . crying, I'm . . . not right, it isn't . . .

(*She quickly wipes her face and smiles*) Why are we not happy? Why have we such a dark view of life? Because our people, the ones we were born to, hated work . . .

(NATALIA IVANOVNA *enters, wearing a pink dress with a green belt.*)

NATASHA: My hair's grand, it's all right.

(*She has seen* IRINA.)

Dear Irina Sergeevna, congratulations. (*Kisses her passionately, at length.*) So many guests you've got. I'm shy, I am . . . Good day, Baron.

(OLGA *enters the drawing room.*)

OLGA: Natalia Ivanovna, she's here. Hello, my dear.

(*They kiss.*)

NATASHA: Happy feast day. So many people here. You entertain so many people – I'm shy, very –

OLGA: Don't be a silly. They're all good friends. (*Lowers her voice, alarmed.*) A green belt, my God, she's wearing a green belt. My dear, that's not good.

NATASHA: Does it bring bad luck, or what – ?

OLGA: No, no, just . . . it's not – it doesn't suit – it looks . . . funny, somehow.

(NATASHA *speaks in a tearful voice.*)

NATASHA: It does? But it's not green – a darker kind of colour, really, it's not . . .

(*She follows* OLGA *into the ballroom where everyone is sitting down. There is no one in the drawing room.*)

KULYGIN: A good husband, Irina, that's what you must find. Time to get married.

CHEBUTYKIN: And it's time you had a serious admirer, Natalia Ivanovna.

KULYGIN: Natalia Ivanovna already has one.

(MASHA *strikes her plate with her fork.*)

MASHA: Wine, wine, wine. To life, sweet life, down but not yet out.

KULYGIN: Four out of ten for good conduct.

VERSHININ: Delicious, this liqueur. What's it made from?

SOLENYI: Cockroaches.

(IRINA *whines.*)

IRINA: No, no, disgusting.

OLGA: Tonight, roast turkey and an apple pie for dinner. I'm home, thank God, all day. Home this evening as well. This evening, you must all come.

VERSHININ: May I be permitted to come this evening?

IRINA: Please do.

NATASHA: Ceremony counts for nothing here.

CHEBUTYKIN: Nature loves us, so she creates us. Why? To love and love – (*He laughs.*)

(ANDREI *reacts angrily.*)

ANDREI: Stop. Do you never tire –

(FEDOTIK *and* RODE *enter, carrying a large basket of flowers.*)

FEDOTIK: See, they're eating already.

(RODE *speaks loudly and in a guttural accent.*)

RODE: Eating? They are, they are . . .

FEDOTIK: Stop, stop everything.

(*Takes a photograph.*)

Two. That's it, finished.

(*They pick up the basket and go into the ballroom. There they are greeted uproariously.*)

RODE: Congratulations. Best wishes, nothing but best wishes. Isn't today wonderful, this mighty weather? All morning we've been working with the boys. I teach gym, the secondary school . . .

FEDOTIK: You can move now, Irina Sergeevna, if you want to.

(*Takes a photograph.*)

You look startling today.

(*Takes a toy top from his pocket.*)

Yes, yes this top, look . . . it makes an extraordinary sound.

IRINA: How beautiful.

MASHA: I saw the shore that strides the sea

A green, green oak, oh green oak tree,

A chain of gold embracing thee –

A chain of gold embracing . . .

(*She speaks plaintively.*) Why do I keep on at that? Why? All this morning it's been in my mind. Why?

KULYGIN: Thirteen at the table. Why? Someone's in love.

(RODE *speaks loudly.*)

RODE: Old wives' tales, who believes them, ladies and gentlemen, does anyone believe –

(*They laugh.*)

CHEBUTYKIN: I'm an old sinner, but I really do not know why Natalia Ivanovna is blushing.

(*They laugh loudly.*

NATASHA *runs out of the ballroom, into the drawing room, followed by* ANDREI.)

ANDREI: Please, please, pay them no attention . . . Wait . . . stop, please.

NATASHA: I'm ashamed of myself . . . What's wrong with me? Why do they make fun of me? It was bad manners on my part to leave the table, but I couldn't . . . couldn't . . .

(*She covers her face with her hands.*)

ANDREI: I beg you, my darling, don't be upset, please. They mean well, honestly, they're only playing. Dear good girl, everyone of them intends us well. They are kind. They're fond of us both. Come on, here to the window, where they can't see us. (*He looks around.*)

NATASHA: I'm not used to society people.

ANDREI: To be young, wonderfully, marvellously young. Dear good girl, don't let this upset you so. Please, believe me . . . so happy . . . I am delighted – my heart loves deeply – they can't see us. They can't. How did I fall in love with you, how? When? I don't know anything. Dear good girl, my

innocent, marry me. I love you. I love you in a way I've never loved anyone –
(*They kiss.*
Two officers enter and, seeing the couple kiss, they stop short in amazement.)

ACT TWO

As in Act One.
It is eight o'clock in the evening. Barely audible, an accordion is being played outside. It is dark.

   NATALIA IVANOVNA *enters wearing a dressing gown, carrying a candle. When she comes in she stops at the door leading to Andrei's room.*

NATASHA: There's no light, is there?
   (ANDREI *enters with a book in his hand.*)
ANDREI: Natasha, what is it?
NATASHA: Looking to see if there was a light. Now the carnival's on, the servants are a bit scatterbrained. You have to keep a sharp eye open in case something happens. Yesterday midnight I walked through the dining room, there was a candle burning. I haven't discovered who lit it. (*Puts down the candle.*) What time is it?
   (*He looks at his watch.*)
ANDREI: Quarter past eight.
NATASHA: Olga and Irina aren't back yet. They haven't come home. Poor things, working, working. Olga's at the teacher's meeting, Irina's still at the telegraph office. (*Sighs.*) Your sister, I said to her, this morning, 'Look after yourself, dear Irina,' I said. She doesn't hear me. Quarter past eight, you say. Bobik is not well at all. He's frozen. Why? He had a temperature yesterday, but he's quite frozen today. I'm worried, very –
ANDREI: Natasha, all's well. The boy's grand.
NATASHA: Still, we better keep an eye on his feed. I'm worried. I'm told the rhymers are coming here around nine. It'd be better if they didn't come, Andrei dear.
ANDREI: I'm not sure. They were asked, you know.
NATASHA: The little dote woke up this morning, he looked at me and all of a sudden, a big smile. You see he recognizes me, he must. I said, 'Bobik, hello. Hello, dote,' and he laughed.

Children know, they know so well. So, Andrei love, I'll tell
them not to allow the rhymers in.

(ANDREI *is indecisive.*)

ANDREI: That's up to my sisters isn't it? It's their house.

NATASHA: Theirs as well, I'll tell them. They're so kind.

(*Going*) For supper I've ordered sour milk. The doctor says
only sour milk for you, or you'll never get thinner. (*Stops*)
Bobik's cold. I'm worried his room might be cold. Shouldn't
he go into another room, at least until the warm weather?
Irina's room, now that is perfect for an infant. It's dry and all
day it gets the sun. For the time being couldn't she share
with Olga? I mean, during the day she is never home, she
only sleeps there.

(*Silence.*)

Andrei, why don't you say anything, my love?

ANDREI: Thinking, just . . . nothing to say really.

NATASHA: Yes. I'd something to tell you. Oh yes. Ferapont's
come from the office. He's asking for you.

(ANDREI *yawns.*)

ANDREI: Send him here.

(NATASHA *exits.*

Stooping over the candle she has forgotten, ANDREI *reads a
book.* FERAPONT *enters, wearing a tatty old overcoat, its collar
turned up, and a scarf tied around his ears.*)

ANDREI: Hello, old boy, what's up?

FERAPONT: The President's sent this big book and some papers.
Here.

(*He hands over the book and packet of papers.*)

ANDREI: Thank you, good. Why did you come so late? It's past
eight o'clock.

FERAPONT: You said?

(ANDREI *speaks louder.*)

ANDREI: I said, you've come late. It's past eight o'clock.

FERAPONT: True. It was still daylight when I got here, they
wouldn't let me see you. Very busy, the master, they said,
well, if he's busy, he's busy, no rush on me.

(*Thinks* ANDREI *has asked him something*) You said?

ANDREI: Nothing.

22

(ANDREI *examines the book.*)

ANDREI: Friday tomorrow, nothing to do. I'll go in anyway, do some work. Home is boring.

(*Silence.*)

Well, old boy, doesn't life change and play strange tricks? Today I was bored and for something to do I picked up this book – old university lectures – funny, it struck me . . . My God, I am secretary of the Rural Office in which office Protopopov presides. I am secretary. At best I can hope to become a member of the local Rural Board, I – I who dream each night that I am a professor of Moscow University, a great academic, the toast of Russia.

FERAPONT: I wouldn't know . . . bad hearing.

ANDREI: Would I talk to you if you could hear me? I must talk to someone. My wife doesn't know me, and my sisters, I'm afraid of them for some reason, afraid, they laugh at me and mock . . . I don't drink, I don't like public houses, but good man, I would like to be sitting in Moscow right now, at Testov's or the Great Moscow.

FERAPONT: The other day at the office this contractor was telling me there were some merchants in Moscow and they were eating pancakes and, the story goes, one of them, he ate forty pancakes and dropped dead. Might have been forty. Might have been fifty. Can't recall.

ANDREI: In Moscow you can sit in the big dining room of a restaurant, nobody knows you, you know nobody, but yet you belong. In this place, here, you know everybody, everybody knows you, yet you don't belong . . . you don't belong, you're on your own.

FERAPONT: You said?

(*Silence.*)

This contractor was telling me – mind you, he mightn't be telling the truth – there's a rope stretched all across Moscow.

ANDREI: Why?

FERAPONT: I can't say. This contractor said it.

ANDREI: Nonsense.

(*Reads the book.*)

Have you ever been to Moscow?

23

(*Silence.*)

FERAPONT: I haven't, no. Not God's will.

(*Silence.*)

Will I leave?

ANDREI: Go, yes. Look after yourself.

(FERAPONT *exits.*)

Look after yourself.

(*Reads.*) Tomorrow morning, come here and fetch some papers . . . Away you go.

(*Silence.*)

He's gone.

(*A bell rings.*)

Yes, work to do.

(*He stretches and goes easily into his room. Offstage the* NANNY *sings a lullaby, rocking the baby to sleep.* MASHA *and* VERSHININ *enter. As they talk a house maid lights the candles and a lamp.*)

MASHA: I don't know.

(*Silence.*)

I don't know. I don't know. I don't know. Of course, habit is important, Take this house, after Father's death. Eventually we had to learn there would be no more orderlies around here. Leaving habit aside, I think I'm justified in what I say. Other places may be different, but in this town, where do you find civilized people? Decent, honourable? In the army.

VERSHININ: I'm parched. I could drink some tea.

(MASHA *glances at her watch.*)

MASHA: They'll bring some soon. When I was eighteen, I was married off. I feared my husband, he was a teacher, I'd just stepped out of school. That was when I imagined he was terribly learned, intelligent, important. It's not like that any more, I'm afraid.

VERSHININ: I see. Yes.

MASHA: I'm not talking about my husband. Him I've got used to. But the civilians here, so many of them are vulgar, rude, bad-mannered people. Vulgarity offends me. It offends me. I'm in pain when I see people lacking refinement, or

24

delicacy, or good manners. With the teachers, my husband's friends, when I'm stuck with them, I squirm, squirm.

VERSHININ: Naturally, but in this town, what difference? Civilians, military are equally without interest. No difference, none. There are educated classes here. Listen to one of them, the same civilians, the same military. His wife wears him out. His house tires him out. His estate, his horses. A loftiness of thought, that's what characterizes the Russian male. So why does he expect so little from life? So very little? Tell me why?

MASHA: Why?

VERSHININ: Why do his wife and children tire him out? Why does he tire out his wife and children?

MASHA: You're a bit depressed today.

VERSHININ: Maybe. I haven't had dinner yet. Since this morning, I've eaten nothing. My daughter's a little pale, and when my little girls are sick, I'm eaten up with worry. Such a mother, my conscience cannot – I wish you'd seen her today. Hateful woman! Seven o'clock in the morning we began to argue. At nine I slammed the door and left.
(*Silence.*)
I don't even talk about it. To you, you alone, do I complain. Isn't that strange? (*Kisses her hand.*) Don't be cross with me. Without you I have no one, no one.
(*Silence.*)

MASHA: The stove, that noise. Just before father died, the chimney howled. Just like that.

VERSHININ: Are you superstitious?

MASHA: Yes.

VERSHININ: Strange. (*Kisses her hand.*) You are a magnificent, marvellous woman. Magnificent and marvellous. It's dark in here, but your eyes, I can see their light.
(MASHA *sits in another chair.*)

MASHA: There's more light here.

VERSHININ: I love you, I love you, I love you. Your eyes, I love the way you move, I dream – magnificent, marvellous woman.
(MASHA *laughs quietly.*)

MASHA: You talk to me like that, and when you do, I laugh. Why? Even as it scares me. Please, don't say it again. (*Speaks low.*) Say it, yes. I don't mind. (*Covers her face with her hands*) I don't mind. Someone's coming. Talk about anything else.

(IRINA *and* TUZENBACH *enter through the ballroom.*)

TUZENBACH: I have a triple-barrelled surname. Baron Tuzenbach-Krone-Altshauer, that's my name. But I'm Russian, of the Orthodox faith. Just like you. There is practically nothing Germanic left in me, except my patience and my persistence, which I bore you with. I walk you home each evening.

IRINA: I am *so* very tired.

TUZENBACH: I'll be at the telegraph office every evening to walk you home. Ten, twenty years, I'll be there, until you chase me away.

(*He notices, with pleasure,* MASHA *and* VERSHININ.)

Hello, it's you.

IRINA: Well, I'm home at last.

(*Talks to* MASHA.) Earlier some woman came in to telegraph her brother in Saratov, her son had died today, but she just couldn't remember the address. She sent it off to Saratov, without any address. She was crying. For no reason at all I was rude to her. 'I have no time for this,' I said. Stupid, stupid thing to do. Are the rhymers coming tonight?

MASHA: Yes.

(IRINA *sits in an armchair.*)

IRINA: Time to rest. I'm tired.

(TUZENBACH *smiles.*)

TUZENBACH: You look so tiny and sad when you come in from work.

IRINA: Tired. I don't like the telegraph office, no, I don't like it.

MASHA: You've grown thinner. (*Whistles*) You look younger as well. Like a boy's, your face.

TUZENBACH: That's because of the way she wears her hair.

IRINA: I must find other work, this doesn't suit me. It lacks what I want, what I dream of so much. It's so prosaic, this work, meaningless.

26

(*There is a knock on the floor.*)

The doctor's knocking.

(To TUZENBACH.) You answer, dear. I can't, I'm tired.

(TUZENBACH *knocks on the floor.*)

He'll be here soon. Look, we must do something. The doctor and Andrei were at the club yesterday. They lost again. It's said Andrei lost two hundred roubles.

(MASHA *is indifferent.*)

MASHA: So? Too late now for us to do anything.

IRINA: He lost a fortnight ago, and lost in December. The sooner he loses everything, the sooner we can escape from this town. Every night I dream of Moscow, I'm like a woman possessed. (*She laughs.*)

Come June, we go there. Until then February, March, April, May – half the year almost.

MASHA: We better see Natasha doesn't find out about the money lost.

IRINA: I don't think she cares.

(CHEBUTYKIN *enters the ballroom. He has been resting after dinner and has just got up. He combs his beard and sits down at the table, taking a newspaper from his pocket.*)

MASHA: Here he comes. Has he paid for his room?

IRINA: Not a penny for eight months. He's simply forgotten, it seems.

(IRINA *laughs. Silence.*)

MASHA: He looks so profound, sitting there.

(*Everyone laughs. Silence.*)

IRINA: Why so quiet, Aleksandr Ignatich?

VERSHININ: I don't know. I need tea. I'd give half my life for a glass of tea. I've eaten nothing since this morning.

CHEBUTYKIN: Irina Sergeevna!

IRINA: Yes?

CHEBUTYKIN: Come here please. *Venez ici.*

(IRINA *goes and sits at the table.*)

I can't manage without you.

(IRINA *lays out the cards for patience.*)

VERSHININ: We're not getting any tea, so be it. Let's start a discussion anyway.

TUZENBACH: Right you be. What about?

VERSHININ: What about? Life, what will it be like when we're dead, imagine it in two or three hundred years' time.

TUZENBACH: All right. We're dead and gone, people will be flying in balloons, fashions will have changed, a sixth sense will be discovered and developed perhaps, but life will be, in essence, the same: difficult, very mysterious, and happy. In a thousand years' time people will still be crying: 'Life, life is hard,' but they'll fear dying and run from death just as they do now.

(VERSHININ *thinks for a moment.*)

VERSHININ: How do I phrase this? I believe all things on earth change, they must, gradually, they are in the process of changing before our eyes. In two hundred, three hundred, even a thousand years – forget the length of time – a new life will emerge, a happy life. We won't be there to share in this life, of course, but we do live for it, we work towards it, and yes, we suffer for it. We are creating it – and that's the point, that is why we exist and why we are happy.

(MASHA *laughs quietly.*)

TUZENBACH: Yes?

MASHA: Nothing. All day I've been laughing. Since morning.

VERSHININ: I went to the same school as you, but I didn't go to the Military Academy. I read plenty but choose books out of ignorance and it's certainly possible that what I read is utterly worthless. But the longer I live, the more I want to know. Look at me, growing grey, practically an old fellow now, yet I know so little, so very little. However, I do know, I think, what is most important, most true. I know it for sure. And I wish so much that I could make you understand that we shall not have happiness, must not, will not ever – our purpose is to work, and work hard, and happiness, that's the fate of generations to come.

(*Silence.*)

Not for me, no, but for my children's children.

(FEDOTIK *and* RODE *appear in the ballroom. They sit down and sing quietly, one of them playing a guitar.*)

TUZENBACH: So you argue that it's pointless even to dream of being happy? Yet what if I am happy?

VERSHININ: No.

(TUZENBACH *clasps his hands and laughs*.)

TUZENBACH: Clearly we don't understand each other. Now, how do I convince you?

(MASHA *laughs softly*. TUZENBACH *holds up a finger to her*.) Laugh on.

(*To* VERSHININ.) Two or three hundred years, a million years pass, and life is still the same as it ever was. It doesn't change, it's constant, it follows its own laws which do not concern you or, at least, you'll never discover what those laws are. Look at migrating birds. Cranes, say. They fly and they fly, it doesn't matter what high or humble thoughts fill their heads, they will simply fly, not knowing where or why. They fly, and they will fly, for all the philosophers in their midst. Certainly let them philosophize, just as long as they're flying.

MASHA: Isn't there some meaning?

TUZENBACH: Meaning? Out there, it's snowing. Does that have a meaning?

(*Silence*.)

MASHA: Man must have faith, I believe, or find a faith, or else it's empty, life is empty. To live and not know why cranes fly, why children are born, why there are stars in the sky . . . You must know why you're living or everything is pointless, empty.

(*Silence*.)

VERSHININ: And yet youth passes and you're sorry to see it passing.

MASHA: What did Gogol say? 'Living in this world is boring, my friends.'

TUZENBACH: What do I say? Arguing with you is hard work, my friends. You're quite –

(CHEBUTYKIN *reads the paper*.)

CHEBUTYKIN: Balzac was married in Berdichev.

(IRINA *sings quietly*.)

Make a note of that.

(*Writes*.)

Balzac was married in Berdichev.

29

(*He reads the newspaper.*

IRINA *plays patience, lost in thought.*)

IRINA: Balzac was married in Berdichev.

TUZENBACH: My fate's decided. You know, Maria Sergeevna, I've resigned my commission.

MASHA: Yes, I've heard and I see nothing good about it. I dislike civilians.

TUZENBACH: All the same.

(*He gets up.*)

What kind of soldier am I? I'm not handsome. It doesn't matter. I'm going to work. For even one day of my life, I will work so hard that when I get home in the evening I will collapse out of sheer exhaustion and I will sleep straight away. Working men sleep soundly, they must.

(*He goes into the ballroom.*

FEDOTIK *speaks to* IRINA.)

FEDOTIK: I've bought you some coloured pencils in Pyzhikov's on Moscow Street. And this tiny knife.

IRINA: You're used to treating me like a little girl, but I'm an adult now, you know. (*Takes the pencils and the knife with delight*) Oh, that's lovely.

FEDOTIK: I bought myself a penknife as well. Look, look. One blade, two blades, three. This one cleans your ears, these are scissors, and this one is for doing your nails.

(RODE *speaks loudly.*)

RODE: Doctor, how old are you?

CHEBUTYKIN: I am thirty-two.

(*Laughter.*)

FEDOTIK: Let me show you another type of patience.

(*The samovar is brought in.* ANFISA *is in charge of it. A moment later* NATASHA *enters and busies herself at the table.* SOLENYI *enters and having bowed to the others, sits down at the table.*)

VERSHININ: This savage wind.

MASHA: Yes. I'm sick of winter. I've even forgotten what summer's like.

IRINA: The cards are going to turn out right, I know it. We will go to Moscow.

FEDOTIK: No, they aren't. Look, the eight was lying on the two of spades. (*Laughs*.) This means you won't go to Moscow.

CHEBUTYKIN: Tsitsekar. Smallpox rages there.

(ANFISA *goes to* MASHA.)

ANFISA: Masha, dear, tea, come along.

(*Addresses* VERSHININ.) Your Excellency, please come. I'm sorry, your name, I've forgotten –

MASHA: Bring it here, nanny. I'm not going over there.

IRINA: Nanny.

ANFISA: Coming, coming.

(NATASHA *talks to* SOLENYI.)

NATASHA: Little babies understand things so clearly. 'Hello, Bobik,' I said, 'Hello, little love,' and he looked at me in that secret way. I'm saying this, you think, because I'm his mother, but no, I assure you, no. He's a wonderful child.

SOLENYI: If that child were mine, I'd eat him. After frying him.

(*He takes his glass into the drawing room and sits down in a corner.* NATASHA *covers her face with her hands*.)

NATASHA: Disgusting, bad mannered man.

MASHA: If people are happy, what difference to them if it's summer or winter? If I were in Moscow I think I wouldn't mind about the weather.

VERSHININ: The other day I was reading the diary of some French politician. He wrote it in prison, the politician, he'd been caught up in the Panama business. He goes into raptures of detail when he sees the birds through his window. He never noticed them before when he was in office. Now he's released, and he no more notices the birds than he ever did. You'll be the same, when you live in Moscow you won't notice it. We are none of us happy, nor can we be. We can only wish to be.

(TUZENBACH *takes a box from the table*.)

TUZENBACH: Where are the sweets?

IRINA: Solenyi ate them.

TUZENBACH: Every one of them?

(ANFISA *serves tea*.)

ANFISA: Sir, a letter for you.

VERSHININ: Me?

(VERSHININ *takes the letter*.)

From my daughter.

(*He reads*.)

Yes, of course. Excuse me, Maria Sergeevna, I'll slip away. I won't have tea. (*Gets up, agitated*) The age-old story again.

MASHA: What is it? Is it a secret?

(VERSHININ *speaks quietly*.)

VERSHININ: My wife's taken poison again. I must leave. I'll go without attracting attention. This is a very unpleasant business.

(*Kisses* MASHA's *hand*.) Dear kind woman, so good . . . I'll slip away from here. (*Exits*.)

ANFISA: Where's he off to? I've brought him his tea. What a strange man.

MASHA: Leave me be. Pestering around me, give me peace. You sicken me, old woman.

ANFISA: How have I offended? Loved one?

(ANDREI *calls offstage*.)

ANDREI: Anfisa.

(ANFISA *mocks him*.)

ANFISA: Anfisa. He's stuck sitting in there –

(*She exits*.

MASHA *is at the table in the ballroom and speaks angrily*.)

MASHA: May I sit down?

(*Mixes up the cards on the table*) Must your cards cover the entire table? Drink your tea.

IRINA: You're somewhat cross, Masha.

MASHA: Well, if I'm somewhat cross, don't speak to me. Don't touch me.

CHEBUTYKIN: Don't touch her, no touching.

MASHA: You are a sixty-year-old man, but the rubbish you constantly come out with, God knows, would suit a bloody schoolboy.

(NATASHA *sighs*.)

NATASHA: Masha, my love, that language, why do you use it in your discourse? I must speak my mind. You have lovely looks and in civilized society you'd be simply charming if it weren't for your language. *Je vous prie, pardonnez-moi,*

32

Marie, mais vous avez des manières un peu grossières.

(TUZENBACH *suppresses his laughter.*)

TUZENBACH: May I . . . may I – the brandy, I think, that's it.

NATASHA: *Il paraît que mon Bobik déjà ne dort pas.* He's awake.
He's been a bit pale today. I'll go to him. Excuse me. (*Exits.*)

IRINA: Where did Aleksandr Ignatich go?

MASHA: He went home. Something's up with his wife. Again.

(TUZENBACH *goes to* SOLENYI *with a decanter of brandy.*)

TUZENBACH: Here you sit, always on your own, brooding over
what – who can tell? Time to make it up. A brandy.
(*They drink.*)
I'll have to thump on the piano all night, I suppose. Any old
rubbish, come what may.

SOLENYI: What do you mean, make it up? I haven't fought with
you.

TUZENBACH: You always make me feel something's wrong
between us. I must say, you're a strange man.
(SOLENYI *recites.*)

SOLENYI: 'So I am strange, so I am strange.
And so who is not strange, strange?
Don't be cross, Aleko.'

TUZENBACH: What's Aleko got to do with it?
(*Silence.*)

SOLENYI: When I'm alone with someone, I'm fine, just like
everyone else. Put me in company, and I'm depressed,
awkward . . . I talk rubbish. Still there's more honesty and
decency in me than in most. I can prove that.

TUZENBACH: You do annoy me often. You can't resist provoking
me in front of people. But I do like you for some reason. No
matter what, I'm getting sozzled tonight. Drink.

SOLENYI: Yes.
(*They drink.*)
I've no grudge against you, Baron. But my personality is like
Lermontov's. (*Lowers his voice*) I have the look of
Lermontov, I've heard say. (*Takes a scent bottle from his
pocket and sprinkles it on his hands.*)

TUZENBACH: I'm resigning my commission. I've had enough.
For five whole years, I've turned this over and over in my

mind and I've made my decision at last. I am going to work.
(SOLENYI *recites*.)

SOLENYI: 'Aleko, don't be angry . . . Forget your dreams, forget.'

(*While they talk* ANDREI *enters quietly with a book and sits down beside the candle.*)

TUZENBACH: I am going to work.

(CHEBUTYKIN *goes into the drawing room with* IRINA.)

CHEBUTYKIN: True Caucasian food it was too. Onion soup, and then, for the meat course, *chechortina*.

SOLENYI: It's not meat, *cheremsha*. It's a vegetable, like an onion.

CHEBUTYKIN: No, no, my angel, *chechortina* isn't an onion, it's roast mutton.

SOLENYI: Listen, *cheremsha* is an onion.

CHEBUTYKIN: What is the point in me arguing with you? You've never been to the Caucasus, you've near eaten *chechortina*.

SOLENYI: I haven't because it sickens me. It stinks like garlic.

ANDREI: Gentlemen, I implore you both, that is enough, please.

TUZENBACH: When do the rhymers come?

IRINA: By nine, they promised. So it's very soon.

(TUZENBACH *embraces* ANDREI. *He begins to sing a folk song.* ANDREI *dances with* TUZENBACH *taking up the song.* CHEBUTYKIN *joins in the song and dance. There is laughter.* TUZENBACH *kisses* ANDREI.)

TUZENBACH: To hell with it, a drink, my loved Andrei, a toast to yourself. I'm going with you, my dearest Andrei, to Moscow when you go to the university.

SOLENYI: Which university? There are two in Moscow.

ANDREI: In Moscow there is *one* university.

SOLENYI: I'm telling you that there are two.

ANDREI: Make it three. The more the merrier.

SOLENYI: There are two universities in Moscow.

(*There are groans and calls for hush.*)

There are two universities in Moscow. An old one and a new one. Perhaps you don't wish to hear me, perhaps what I say annoys you, well I can stop speaking. I can even leave the room and go elsewhere. (*Exits through one of the doors.*)

TUZENBACH: More, more. (*Laughs.*) Friends, let us commence.

Now I shall sit and play. Solenyi, that strange –
(*He sits at the piano and plays a waltz which* MASHA *dances alone to.*)

MASHA: The Baron is drunk, is drunk.
       The Baron is drunk, is drunk, is drunk . . .
       (NATASHA *enters.*)

NATASHA: Ivan Romanych.
       (*She speaks to* CHEBUTYKIN *and then quietly exits.*
       CHEBUTYKIN *touches* TUZENBACH's *shoulder and whispers to him.*)

IRINA: What's wrong?

CHEBUTYKIN: We must go, time to go. Mind yourselves.

TUZENBACH: Goodnight. Time to go.

IRINA: Why? What about the rhymers?
       (ANDREI *is embarrassed.*)

ANDREI: The rhymers aren't coming. It's because Bobik isn't
       very well, my dear. Natasha says. I don't know and, well, I
       don't care.
       (IRINA *shrugs her shoulders.*)

IRINA: Bobik isn't very well.

MASHA: So why are we punished? Well, if we're being shown the
       door, through the door we must go. It isn't Bobik who's sick.
       She is – up here. (*Taps her forehead with her finger*) Silly little
       shopgirl.
       (ANDREI *goes to his room through the door on his right.*
       CHEBUTYKIN *follows him. Farewells are exchanged in the
       ballroom.*)

FEDOTIK: How sad. I had thought I'd spend the evening here,
       but if the baby's not well, of course . . . I'll bring him a toy
       tomorrow.
       (RODE *speaks loudly.*)

RODE: I went and had a good sleep after dinner today. I thought
       I'd be dancing all night. It's only just gone nine o'clock.

MASHA: Outside, everyone, come on. We can say what we like out
       there. We'll decide what to do.
       (*'Goodbyes' sound offstage, and cries of 'take care'.*
       TUZENBACH *laughs cheerfully.* ANFISA *and the housemaid clear
       the table and put out the lights.*)

The child's NANNY *sings offstage.* ANDREI *enters quietly, in coat and hat, accompanied by* CHEBUTYKIN.)

CHEBUTYKIN: I'd no luck in the marriage stakes, and my life's passed like a flash of lightning. Anyway, I loved your mother like a man possessed, and she was married.

ANDREI: Don't marry. Don't. Why not? It's boring.

CHEBUTYKIN: Perhaps, but so is being on your own. Say what you like, to be alone is terrible, old boy . . . although, when it comes down to it, of course it doesn't make a whit of difference.

ANDREI: Get a move on.

CHEBUTYKIN: What's your rush? We'll get there.

ANDREI: I'm afraid my wife might stop me.

CHEBUTYKIN: Ah.

ANDREI: I won't bet tonight, I'll just sit and watch, I'm not well. Have you a cure for shortness of breath, Ivan Romanych?

CHEBUTYKIN: Don't ask me. I've forgotten, old boy. I don't know.

ANDREI: We'll go through the kitchen.

(*They exit.*
There is the sound of a bell, then another. Voices and laughter are heard.

IRINA *enters.*)

IRINA: What's that?

(ANFISA *whispers.*)

ANFISA: The rhymers.

(*The bell sounds.*)

IRINA: Nanny, there's no one home, tell them. We apologize, tell them.

(ANFISA *exits.*
IRINA *walks about the room, lost in thought and agitated.*
SOLENYI *enters, in bewilderment.*)

SOLENYI: No one's here. Where are they all?

IRINA: Gone. Home.

SOLENYI: Strange. Are you on your own?

IRINA: Yes.

(*Silence.*)
Goodbye.

SOLENYI: I lost control of myself earlier. I behaved badly. You . . .
you are not like the rest of them. You are far above them. You
are pure. You see truth. You, and you alone, could succeed in
understanding me. I love you from the depth of my being, my
love is infinite.

IRINA: Goodbye. Get out.

SOLENYI: I cannot exist without you.
(*Comes after her.*) My joy, my joy. (*Speaks through his tears.*)
My happiness. Your eyes, they're glorious, they weave a spell,
they astonish, in no other woman have I seen such eyes.
(IRINA *is cold.*)

IRINA: Enough, Vasilii Vasil'evich.

SOLENYI: For the first time I have spoken to you about love, and
I am not on this earth, I feel on some other planet. (*Rubs his
forehead*) But that is immaterial. I can't demand that you be
tender, of course. Still, I won't tolerate any more pleasing
rivals. That I will not have. By all that's sacred, I give you
my oath that I will kill any rival. So wonderful, you are so
wonderful.
(NATASHA *enters with a candle. She looks through one door, then
another, bypassing the door to her husband's room.*)

NATASHA: Andrei's in there. Leave him be to read. I didn't know
you were here, Vasilii Vasil'evich, forgive me. I'm wearing
my housecoat.

SOLENYI: Who cares? Goodbye. (*Exits.*)

NATASHA: My love, my sweet little girl, who's tired? (*Kisses
IRINA.*) Go to bed earlier, you must.

IRINA: Is Bobik sleeping?

NATASHA: He is but he's not sleeping peacefully. Darling,
something I've been trying to ask you, but you either haven't
been around or I've been so busy – I think it's nasty and
damp in Bobik's room. Now your room, it would be perfect
for a baby. Dearest, would you move in with Olga just for
the present?
(IRINA *does not understand.*)

IRINA: Where?
(*A troika with bells can be heard drawing up to the house.*)

NATASHA: Olga's room, for the next while, you could go in there

37

and Bobik can take your room. He's such a little flirt. I said
to him today: 'You're mine, Bobik, all mine.' And he gazed
straight at me with his little eyes, so sweet.
(*The bell sounds.*)
That has to be Olga. She's very late, isn't she?
(*The housemaid comes to* NATASHA *and whispers to her.*)
Protopopov? He's a funny fellow, isn't he? Protopopov's
arrived and he wants me to drive with him, in a troika.
(*Laughs*) Men. Strange beings, aren't they?
(*The bell sounds.*)
Someone's here, I could manage a fifteen-minute drive. Tell
him I'm on my way.
(*The bell sounds.*)
They're ringing the bell. Olga, it must be. (*Exits.*)
(*The housemaid runs off.*

IRINA *sits thinking.* KULYGIN *enters with* OLGA, VERSHININ
following her.)

KULYGIN: What's going on here? Didn't they say they were
having a party?
VERSHININ: Funny! I can't have left more than half an hour ago,
they were waiting then for the rhymers.
IRINA: They've gone, all of them.
KULYGIN: Masha, she's gone as well? Where's she gone to?
Protopopov's downstairs, in a troika. Why? He's waiting.
Who for?
IRINA: Don't bother me with questions. I'm exhausted.
KULYGIN: Spoiled child.
OLGA: We've just finished the meeting. I'm worn down. Our
headmistress is ill, I've to step in for the moment. My head,
my head is opening, my head. (*Sits down.*) Two hundred
roubles, Andrei lost them at the cards yesterday. The entire
town is talking about it.
KULYGIN: Yes, the meeting exhausted me too.
VERSHININ: Well, my wife got the bright idea of scaring me to
death. She nearly poisoned herself. All's well now, I'm glad
to report, I can relax. So, it's time to leave? Right, I'll make
my farewells. Fedor Il'ich, let's go out somewhere. Tonight I
can't be at home, I simply cannot. Let's go out.

38

KULYGIN: I'm tired, I'm going nowhere. (*Stands up.*) Tired. My
wife, she's gone home?

IRINA: Where else?

(KULYGIN *kisses* IRINA's *hand.*)

KULYGIN: Goodbye. All day tomorrow, and the day after, we can
rest. My best wishes. (*Moves to go.*) I'm longing for a drink of
tea. I hoped to be spending this evening in lively company
but – *O fallacem hominum spem.* Accusative's in order when
you make your exclamation.

VERSHININ: So. I'll go off on my own somewhere. (*Exits,
whistling, with* KULYGIN.)

OLGA: My head, my head, pain – Andrei lost – the entire town
talking – I'm going to lie down. (*Rises.*) Tomorrow, I'm
free . . . sweet God, thank you . . . Tomorrow, I'm free, and
the day after . . . My head, pain, my head. (*Exits.*)

IRINA: They're all gone. No one is here.

(*An accordion plays outside.*
The NANNY *sings a song.*
Followed by a housemaid, NATASHA, *in a fur coat and hat,*
crosses the ballroom.)

NATASHA: I'll be home in half an hour. I'll just have a little drive.

(IRINA, *left alone, speaks with longing in her voice.*)

IRINA: Moscow. Moscow. Moscow.

ACT THREE

Olga's and Irina's bedroom. There are two beds, to left and right, behind screens. It has gone two in the morning. Offstage an alarm bell rings because a fire has been raging for a long time already. It is clear that no one in the house has gone to bed yet. Dressed, as usual, in black, MASHA *lies on the sofa.*

OLGA *and* ANFISA *enter.*

ANFISA: There they are sitting on the stairs down below . . . I said to them, get up those stairs, you can't sit here, but they kept crying. Our daddy, where is he, we don't know, they said, he might be all burned. What a thing to get into their heads. And there's some people out in the yard – they have barely a stitch on their backs.

(OLGA *takes clothes from the cupboard.*)

OLGA: This grey thing, take it . . . and this . . . the blouse as well . . . this skirt too, Nanny. Sweet God, it's terrible. Kirsanovskii Street, burnt entirely to the ground, it seems . . . Take this . . . and this. (*Flings clothes into* ANFISA's *arms.*) The poor Vershinins had the fright of their life. Their house had a lucky escape from the fire. They'll have to sleep here tonight, we can't let them go home. Poor Fedotik, everything's burnt, he's lost the lot.

ANFISA: We'll have to call Ferapont, Olga dear, I can't manage all this.

(OLGA *rings the bell.*
A window, red with fire, can be seen through the open door. The fire brigade is heard passing the house.)

OLGA: Not a being's answering. (*Calls through the door.*) If there's anyone about, get in here. How terrible it is, terrible, and how tired I am.

(FERAPONT *enters.*)

Take this downstairs. The Kolotilin girls are under the stairs. Give this to them. And give this to them too.

FERAPONT: Yes, Miss. In 1812 Moscow burnt to the ground.

God above. The French got a warm welcome.

OLGA: Move, move.

FERAPONT: Yes.

OLGA: Nanny dear, give the lot away. What need have we for any of it? Give the lot away, Nanny. I'm tired, I can hardly stay on my feet. We can't let the Vershinins go home. The little girls can sleep in the drawing room. Aleksandr Ignatich can go downstairs with the Baron. Fedotik can go in with the Baron too, unless he goes into our ballroom. The doctor's drunk, ridiculously drunk, you'd almost swear he did it on purpose, we daren't put anybody in his room. Vershinin's wife can go into the drawing room as well.

(ANFISA *speaks wearily*.)

ANFISA: My own darling Olga, don't send me away. Don't, please.

OLGA: You're being silly, Nanny. Nobody's sending you away.

(ANFISA *lays her head against* OLGA's *breast*.)

ANFISA: I love you, I treasure you, I work, I work, I *do*. My strength's going, they'll order me out. Where in this world can I go? Where? I'm eighty years old. I'll be eighty-two –

OLGA: Nanny, sit down. You're worn out, poor thing. (*Sits* ANFISA *down*.) Take a little rest, loved one. You're very pale.

(NATASHA *enters*.)

NATASHA: They say a fund should be started without delay to help the victims of the fire. Why not? A magnificent gesture. It's right that the rich should help the poor. Bobik and Sifochka are asleep, sound as bells, as if nothing happened. The house is packed with people. No matter where you go, it's crowded. There's flu in the town just now. I'm in a panic the children might catch it.

(OLGA *is not listening to her*.)

OLGA: From this room you can't see the fire. So peaceful, here.

NATASHA: Yes. I'm sure my hair is all over the place. (*Looks in the mirror*.) People say I'm getting fatter, and that's not true. Not in the slightest. Masha's sleeping, she's spent, the poor girl. (*Speaks coldly to* ANFISA) Do you dare sit down in my presence? Get up. Get out of here.

(ANFISA *exits*.

Silence.)

42

For the life of me I cannot understand why you tolerate that
old woman.

(OLGA *is taken aback*.)

OLGA: I'm sorry, I cannot understand you, either –

NATASHA: Good for nothing, that's what she is here. A peasant.
She should be back living in the sticks. Why spoil her, why?
Give me order about the house. There's no point in having
useless people around. (*Strokes* OLGA's *cheek*.) Poor thing,
you're tired. Our headmistress is tired. When my little
Sophie becomes a big girl and goes to secondary school, I'll
be frightened of you.

OLGA: I'm not going to be a headmistress.

NATASHA: Olga dear, you will be chosen, that is that.

OLGA: I'll turn it down. I can't . . . my strength's not up to it.
(*Drinks some water*.) You spoke so savagely to Nanny just
now. Forgive me, I can't endure it, I thought I'd faint.

(NATASHA *is agitated*.)

NATASHA: Olia, forgive me, forgive me . . . I didn't mean to hurt
you . . .

(MASHA *gets up, takes a pillow and exits angrily*.)

OLGA: Please understand, dear. We may have had an unusual
upbringing, but I will not stand for that. That kind of
behaviour depresses me, it makes me ill . . . it just shocks
me.

NATASHA: Forgive me, forgive me. (*Kisses* OLGA.)

OLGA: Any sign of rudeness upsets me, even the smallest, any
hard words –

NATASHA: It's true I can and do say too much, but you must
admit, darling, she should go back and live in the country.

OLGA: She's been with us now for thirty years.

NATASHA: And she cannot work any more! Either I don't
understand you or you won't understand me. She's not up to
working. She's either snoozing or sitting about.

OLGA: Then let her sit about.

(NATASHA *is surprised*.)

NATASHA: Did you say, let her sit about? The woman is a *servant*.
(*Speaks through tears*.) Olia, I don't understand you. I have a
nanny and a wet-nurse. We employ a maid and a cook. Why

43

do we need this old woman as well? Why?

(*The alarm sounds offstage*.)

OLGA: I must have aged ten years this night.

NATASHA: Olia, I demand we come to some clear arrangement.
Firm and final. You go to the school, I stay at home. You
teach, I run the house. When I say something about the
servants, then I know what I'm talking about. I know what
I'm talking about. That old robber, that wizzened hag –
(*Stamps her feet*.) That witch, she will walk out this door
tomorrow. You, do not dare cross me. You, do not dare.
(*Gets a grip on herself*.) Honestly, you should go downstairs,
or we'll just keep on arguing. It's dreadful.

(KULYGIN *enters*.)

KULYGIN: Is Masha here? It's high time we went home. They say
the fire's dying down. (*Stretches*.) Only one part of the town
got burned down, but when that wind started up, it looked
likely at first the whole place would go. (*Sits down*.) I'm worn
out. My dear good Olga, had it not been for Masha I often
think I would have married you, dearest Olga. So good, you
are . . . I'm worn out. (*Listens*.)

OLGA: What is it?

KULYGIN: He's drunk, the doctor, on purpose, almost,
ridiculously drunk. On purpose almost. (*Gets up*.) He's
coming in here, I think . . . Do you hear him? . . . Yes, in he
comes. (*Laughs*) What a character, honestly. I'm going to
hide. (*Goes into the corner by the cupboard*.) What a rascal.

OLGA: Off the drink for two years, then just like that, he goes and
gets drunk.

(*She and* NATASHA *go to the back of the room*.

CHEBUTYKIN *enters. He crosses the room without staggering, as
if sober. He stops, looks about, goes to the wash-stand and
washes his hands. He speaks glumly*.)

CHEBUTYKIN: The devil take them, everyone of them . . . damn
them . . . because I'm a doctor they think I can heal
everything, but I know nothing, nothing, everything I know
I've forgotten. I remember not one thing. Nothing, nothing.
(*He does not notice* OLGA *and* NATASHA *exit*.)
The devil take them. Wednesday last I attended a woman in

Zasyp. Died she did. I am to blame for her dying. Yes . . . I knew something, twenty years ago, but now not a thing do I remember. Not a thing . . . Empty head, and I don't care. I may not be a man at all. I may be just pretending I have arms and legs . . . and a head. I may not exist at all, I only think I am walking, eating, sleeping. (*Weeps*.) Oh, let me not be. (*Stops crying and speaks glumly*.) God alone knows. The day before yesterday, at the club, they were having a conversation. They were talking about Shakespeare, Voltaire. I have never read them. Not one word. But my face looked as if I had. The others looked like me. How low, how hateful. And I remembered that woman that I had killed last Wednesday. I remembered it all . . . and I felt deformed, and wicked, and stuffed with self hatred . . . so I went off and I got stupid drunk.

(IRINA, VERSHININ *and* TUZENBACH *enter*.

TUZENBACH *wears new and fashionable civilian clothes*.)

IRINA: We'll sit down for a while. No one will come in here.

VERSHININ: The whole town would have burned to ashes if it hadn't been for the soldiers. Good lads. (*Rubs his hands with pleasure*.) First class, these men. Yes, yes, they're good lads.

(KULYGIN *goes up to them*.)

KULYGIN: What's the time?

TUZENBACH: Past three o'clock. It's getting light.

IRINA: They're all sitting in the ballroom. No one's leaving. Your very own Solenyi is stuck in there too. Doctor, do go to bed.

CHEBUTYKIN: I am fine . . . thank you.

(KULYGIN *laughs*.)

KULYGIN: Light in the head, eh, Ivan Romanych? (*Slaps* CHEBUTYKIN's *shoulders*) Fine man. *In vino veritas*, so the ancients say.

TUZENBACH: They keep asking me to arrange a concert to help the victims of the fire.

IRINA: So who could be in it?

TUZENBACH: We could arrange it, if we wanted. Maria Sergeevna, for one, she plays piano quite wonderfully.

KULYGIN: Yes, she plays wonderfully.

IRINA: She'll have forgotten how to by now. She hasn't played for three years . . . or four.

45

TUZENBACH: There is not a single being, not one soul, in this town who can understand music. Now I, I do understand it and I tell you emphatically that Maria Sergeevna is an excellent pianist. Almost inspired.

KULYGIN: Quite right, Baron. I'm extremely fond of Masha. She is splendid.

TUZENBACH: To have the power to play so wonderfully, and yet know, all the time, not one soul, not one, understands.

(KULYGIN *sighs*.)

KULYGIN: Yes . . . Do you think it would be all right for her to participate in a concert?

(*Silence.*)

Of course, friends, I myself know nothing about it. Perhaps it would be acceptable. I must say this, our headmaster, a good man, a fine man even, very, very intelligent, yes, but he does have certain opinions . . . Of course, this in no way concerns him, but all the same I could have a few words with him, if you like.

(CHEBUTYKIN *picks up a china clock and examines it*.)

VERSHININ: The fire covered me in filth. I look like nothing on earth.

(*Silence.*)

I caught word yesterday they might transfer the brigade somewhere far away. Poland, some say, or Chita.

TUZENBACH: So I heard as well. It will be a ghost town then.

IRINA: Then we leave too.

(CHEBUTYKIN *drops the clock, breaking it in pieces*.)

CHEBUTYKIN: Broken into bits.

(*Silence. Everyone is embarrassed and upset*.)

KULYGIN: Dropping such a valuable object. Ivan Romanych, dear me, Ivan Romanych, E-minus for conduct.

IRINA: Mama owned the clock.

CHEBUTYKIN: That may be true . . . if Mama owned it, Mama owned it. And yet I may not have broken it, it's just illusion that I did. It may also be just illusion that we exist, when if the truth were told, we don't. I do not know anything. Nobody knows anything.

(*At the door*.) What are you looking at? Natasha is having her

46

way with Protopopov. And you don't notice . . . You sit
here, you see nothing, and Natasha has her way with
Protopopov.
(*Sings*) This sweet-smelling fruit I give you . . .
(*Exits.*)

VERSHININ: Indeed, hah. (*Laughs*) Very odd, yes, isn't it?
(*Silence.*)
When the fire started, I made for home as fast as my feet
could carry me. When I came to our house, I saw it still
standing, out of harm's way, no danger, but there they were,
my two little girls, in the doorway, standing in their
nightclothes. No mother to be seen, people all over the place,
horses and dogs let loose . . . Their two faces, all alarmed,
dreading, begging – what for I don't know. Sweet God, I
thought, these little girls, they will live a long time and what
will they go through? I lifted them in my arms and I ran and
all I could ask was, what will they have to endure in this
world?
(*The alarm sounds.*
Silence.)
I came here. There was Mother. Roaring her head off.
Furious.
(MASHA *enters with a pillow and sits on the sofa.*)
My little girls when they were standing in the doorway, in
just their nightclothes, their feet bare, the street scarlet with
fire, the noise, the noise, I suddenly realized this is what
must have happened many years ago; the enemy attacked,
started looting, burning. Yet, how different, in their reality,
these times are from those times. And before too long, in
three hundred years, say, the way we live now will be looked
back on with horror and contempt. Things as they are today
will seem awkward and hard, odd and graceless. Yes, yes,
life, that life, will be so . . . so full. (*Laughs*) I ask your
forgiveness. Philosophy, too much of it again, that's me.
Friends, let me go on. I will die if I don't philosophize. Right
now, I'm in the mood.
(*Silence.*)
Are you all asleep? It seems so . . . Yet I was saying, life will

47

be full. In this town, at the present moment, there are only three like you. Now, imagine it, try. Time passes, there will be others like you. More, many more of them. Time will come when all will be changed and be changed as you would wish it, people will live the way you would wish them to live. And then with more time you will be surpassed – people will be born who are better than you. (*Laughs*) I'm in a powerful mood this day. I wish to be wicked, drink, live.
(*Sings*) Love's the burden on us all,

Love is pain, love is fall –
(MASHA *takes up the song, 'la-la-ing'.* VERSHININ *continues, 'dum-dumming'.* MASHA *questions with a 'la-la'.* VERSHININ *replies with a 'dum-de-dum'. He laughs.* FEDOTIK *enters, dancing.*)

FEDOTIK: Ash to ash and dust to dust. Cleaned out entirely.
(*They laugh.*)

IRINA: This is not a joke. Is everything burnt?
(FEDOTIK *laughs.*)

FEDOTIK: Cleaned out entirely. Nothing left. Guitar burnt. Photographic equipment burnt. All my letters . . . A little notebook I was going to give you – burnt, burnt.
(SOLENYI *enters.*)

IRINA: Will you please leave, Vasilii Vasil'ich, I do not wish you in here.

SOLENYI: The Baron's allowed in, I am not, why?

VERSHININ: We should be going. How's the fire?

SOLENYI: Dying down, they say. No, it seems decidedly odd to me, the Baron's allowed in, not me, Why?
(*He takes out a scent bottle and sprinkles himself.*
VERSHININ *continues the song.* MASHA *picks it up.* VERSHININ *laughs and speaks to* SOLENYI.)

VERSHININ: Come on, the ballroom.

SOLENYI: As you say. We'll mark this down. 'Were I to make my meaning plain, the goosie-gander would squeal with pain.'
(*He looks at* TUZENBACH) Cheep, cheep, cheep. (*Exits with* VERSHININ *and* FEDOTIK.)

IRINA: That Solenyi has filled the room with smoke. (*Puzzled*) The Baron's sleeping. Baron, Baron.

48

(TUZENBACH *wakes up*.)

TUZENBACH: Tired, I must – . The brickworks. Not sleep-talking, no. I really must go down to the brickworks. Start work. Discussed it already.

(*Speaks tenderly to* IRINA) So pale you are, full of beauty, bewitching, so – you're pale and you light the darkness, it surrounds you. Sad you are, you're not happy in this life – come, live with me and be my fellow worker.

MASHA: Nikolai L'vovich, leave.

(TUZENBACH *laughs*.)

TUZENBACH: You're here? I didn't see you. (*Kisses* IRINA'*s hand*.) Bye-bye, I go. I'm looking at you, and yes, it's a long time ago, but I do remember your feast day, the party, you are lively, full of cheer, and you talk of working, the joys . . . What a happy life I imagined I'd have then. Where's it gone? (*Kisses her hand*.) In your eyes there are tears. Bed, go. It's nearly light. The morning begins . . . If I could lay down my life for you, if only –

MASHA: Nikolai L'vovich, leave. Please . . .

TUZENBACH: Going, going.

(*He exits.*

MASHA *lies down*.)

MASHA: Fedor, are you asleep?

KULYGIN: What?

MASHA: Go home, do, go on. Yes?

KULYGIN: My sweet Masha, my sweet Masha . . .

IRINA: She's worn out. Let her rest, Fedia –

KULYGIN: In a minute, I'll go. Wife, lovely, my sweet, you, I love . . . I love –

MASHA: *Amo, amas, amat, amamus, amatis, amant.*

(KULYGIN *laughs*.)

KULYGIN: No, well now, isn't she beyond belief? Seven years I've been married to you, but do you know it seems like yesterday we married. No really, the woman is beyond belief. Happy, happy, I am happy.

MASHA: Bored, bored, I am bored.

(*She sits up.*)

Something's preying on my mind. I can't get rid of it. It's an

49

outright disgrace. It's driving a nail through my head, I cannot keep silent. Andrei, Andrei . . . he's mortgaged the house to a bank. His wife's got her claws on the money. All of it. The house is not his alone, is it? It belongs to all four of us, yes? Does he not know this? Is he not a decent man?

KULYGIN: Masha, why do you bring this up? What's wrong with you? Dearest Andrei is in debt right, left, and centre, God help him.

MASHA: It's a disgrace, either way.

(*She lies down.*)

KULYGIN: Are we poor? No. I work, I go to the secondary school, and then there's the private lessons I give. I'm an honest man. Simple. *Omnia mea mecum porto*, as they say.

MASHA: I want nothing. It is the lack of justice which revolts me.

(*Silence.*)

Leave, Fedor.

(KULYGIN *kisses her.*)

KULYGIN: Tired out, aren't you? Rest yourself for half an hour, and I'll wait for you out there. Sleep, sleep.

(*He is going.*)

Happy, happy, I'm happy. (*Exits.*)

IRINA: That woman, poor Andrei has turned into such a fool since he's been with her. He's lost his way, he's aged so much, so much. Time was he was preparing to be a professor. Yesterday he was showing off that he'd succeeded, at long last, in becoming a member of the Rural Board. A member of the board he is, and Protopopov is president. The entire town is talking and sniggering. He's the only one who knows nothing. He doesn't see. Everyone racing to the fire, he sits there in his room, he doesn't notice a thing. No, he plays the violin. (*Edgy*) It is hideous, yes. Hideous, hideous. (*Weeps*) No more, take no more. Cannot, cannot. Cannot, cannot.

(OLGA *enters and tidies the table.*

IRINA *sobs loudly.*)

Order me out, order me out of the house. I cannot go on.

(OLGA *is frightened.*)

OLGA: What's wrong, what's wrong, loved one?

(IRINA *sobs*.)

IRINA: Where? I'm asking where it's gone? Where? God, sweet God, it's all forgotten. I've forgotten, my head – everything tangled – Italian, I don't remember their word for window, or for ceiling – I'm forgetting everything, every day I forget something and life's passing . . . it's going and it won't give back – never ever – we'll not go to Moscow, ever – I see it, we won't go –

OLGA: Loved one, loved one –
(IRINA *keeps a grip on herself*.)

IRINA: Silly, silly. Can't work. Won't work. Enough is enough. I was in the post office, now I'm working in the town council. I hate and I hinder every item of work I'm given to do. I'm twenty-three, I've been working for ages now, and my brain's drying up. I'm getting thinner, I'm getting ugly, old, old, what have I to show for it? I have no satisfaction, none. And time's passing. I don't know where I am but I am moving further and further away from a good, genuine life. This is a pit I am in. I am in hell. I am in despair. Why am I still alive? Why have I not killed myself? I don't know.

OLGA: Good child, stop crying. Stop crying. It hurts me.

IRINA: I'm not crying now. Enough. Do you see, not crying? Enough, enough.

OLGA: Loved one, I'm your sister, I'm your friend, listen to me. Do you want my advice? Marry the Baron.
(IRINA *cries quietly*.)
You respect him, you value him, you know that. It's true he's not good-looking. But he is decent, he is good. Who marries for love? They do their duty. At least that's what I think. And I would marry without being in love. If the man was decent, I would get married no matter what. I'd even marry an old man.

IRINA: All this while I've been waiting for us to move to Moscow. There alone I would meet my true love, I've dreamt of him, loved him. But it's all mockery, it's turned out a mockery.
(OLGA *embraces her sister*.)

OLGA: My beautiful sister, I know. When Baron Nikolai L'vovich resigned and came to see us dressed as a civilian, he looked so

51

plain, I could have cried. I did. He asked me, why are you crying? What could I answer him? But if it were God's will he marries you, I'd be happy. That would be different, very different.

(NATASHA *crosses the stage from right-hand door to left, carrying a candle, not speaking.*

MASHA *sits up.*)

MASHA: There she blows, and you'd swear she started the fire.

OLGA: Masha, you are an idiot. I hope you will excuse me for saying this, but in this family, you are the idiot.

(*Silence.*)

MASHA: My loved sisters, I have something to tell you. My heart is in my mouth. I'm going to tell you, and you only. I'm going to say it now.

(*Speaks quietly*) It's my big secret, I want you to know everything. I can't keep it quiet.

(*Silence.*)

I'm in love. In love. I love that man you've just seen. Vershinin. I'm in love.

(OLGA *goes behind her screen.*)

OLGA: Stop. I will not hear any more about it. Don't.

MASHA: What can I do? (*Holds her head.*) At the beginning I thought him odd, then I felt sorry . . . then I fell in love with him . . . His voice, in love with it, his words, his unhappiness, yes, his two little girls . . .

(OLGA *speaks from behind her screen.*)

OLGA: I will not hear it, I refuse, no. Talk any nonsense you want, go ahead. I will not hear it.

MASHA: Idiot Olia, idiot. I love him – I have to, I must. The die is cast. And he loves me. So terrifying, all of this. Isn't it? Not very good, is it?

(*She takes* IRINA *by the hand and draws her close.*)

Sweet woman, what's to become of us? What about our lives? When you read novels, you think this is so familiar. The same old story. Then, fall in love yourself, and you –

(*Silence.*)

No one knows anything for certain.

(*Silence.*)

But you have to make up your own mind. Loved sisters, my sisters, I've said my piece to you, now I'll be silent, like the lunatic in Gogol, the madman . . . Silence . . . silence.

(ANDREI *enters, followed by* FERAPONT. *He speaks angrily.*)

ANDREI: What is it you want? I don't understand.

(FERAPONT *stands in the doorway. He is impatient.*)

FERAPONT: Ten times have I told you, Andrei Sergeich.

ANDREI: For a start, I am not Andrei Sergeich to your likes. I am your Honour.

FERAPONT: The firemen are asking will you let them drive through the garden to get to the river, your Honour. They have to keep going round. It's a terrible bother.

ANDREI: All right. Tell them all right.

(FERAPONT *exits.*)

Where's Olga?

(OLGA *comes from behind the screen.*)

I've come to ask you for the key to the cupboard. I've lost mine. You have that little key.

(OLGA *silently gives him the key.*

IRINA *goes behind her screen.*

Silence.)

That fire, colossal. It's dying down now. Ferapont, damn him, he annoyed me. What I said to him was stupid . . . your Honour . . .

(*Silence.*)

Olia, why are you not speaking?

(*Silence.*)

It's about time an end was put to this stupidity, this sulking for no reason. Stop it. You're here, Masha, Irina's here, excellent. Let's have it out, once and for all. What have you got against me? What?

OLGA: Dear Andrei, no more. Tomorrow, we'll talk.

(*Agitated*) This night, it's awful.

(ANDREI *is very embarrassed.*)

ANDREI: No need to be upset. I am only asking you. What have you got against me? Speak out.

(VERSHININ's *voice is heard singing, 'dum-de-dum'.*

MASHA *rises and replies loudly to the song.*)

MASHA: La-la-la. Olia, goodbye. God bless you.

(She goes behind the screen and kisses IRINA.)

Sleep tight. Goodbye, Andrei. Let them be. They're worn out. Tomorrow, we'll talk. *(Exits.)*

OLGA: Come on, Andrei dear, let it rest until tomorrow.

(Goes behind her screen.) Time we slept.

ANDREI: I'll say this, and this only, then I'll leave. Just one moment . . . For a start, Natasha, my wife, you've something against her. I've sensed it since our wedding day. That is my opinion. I love, and I respect, my wife – know that. I respect her. I demand others also respect her. I repeat that she is an honest person, decent, and if you are not satisfied with her, then it is because – you are up to mischief – forgive me saying so.

(Silence.)

Another thing, you seem to be cross that I'm not a professor and avoid doing anything academic. Look, I serve on the council, I'm a member of the Rural Board, and this service is as valuable, it is as important as anything academic. I am a member of the Rural Board, I am proud of it, if you'd like to know . . .

(Silence.)

A third thing . . . there is something else to tell you. I mortgaged the house, I didn't ask your permission. I stand accused on that, I ask your pardon. Debt, my debt, forced me – thirty-five thousand . . . I no longer play cards, I gave it up years ago. The most important thing though I have to say in my defence – the girls, you, receive an allowance, while I have nothing – no income, so to speak.

(Silence.

KULYGIN *speaks through the door.)*

KULYGIN: Is Masha not here?

(Worried.) Where's she gone then? Strange. *(Exits.)*

ANDREI: They're not listening. An excellent person, Natasha, honest.

(He walks about the stage in silence, then he stops.) I married her and I thought we would be happy, all of us, happy. But, sweet God – *(Weeps)* Sisters, my dear sisters, don't believe

54

what I say, don't believe it. (*Exits.*)
(KULYGIN *calls through the door.*)

KULYGIN: Where's Masha? Masha's not here, is she? Strange.
(*Exits.*)
(*The alarms sounds.*
The stage is empty.)

IRINA: Olia, who's knocking on the floor?

OLGA: The doctor, Ivan Romanych, drunk.

IRINA: This dark night.
(*Silence.*)
Olia?
(*Looks from behind the screens.*) Have you heard? The
brigade's being moved from here. They're being posted
somewhere far away.

OLGA: Hearsay, only hearsay.

IRINA: We'll be on our own then. Olga?

OLGA: What?

IRINA: My dear, I respect the Baron, I do, I value him. A good
man. I will marry him, I will accept, but we must go to
Moscow. I beseech you, we must go. Moscow, there's
nowhere better on this earth. We must go, Olia. We must go.

ACT FOUR

The old garden attached to the Prozorov house.
There is a long avenue of fir trees, at the end of which a river is visible.
On the far side of the river is a forest. The veranda of the house is to the
right, and there is a table with bottles and glasses. They have evidently
been drinking champagne. It is midday. Every so often people come
through the garden from the street, going to the river. Five or six soldiers
march by sharply. CHEBUTYKIN, *in an affable mood which does not*
desert him throughout the act, sits in an armchair, waiting to be
summoned. He wears his army cap and has a walking stick. KULYGIN
wears a decoration round his neck and is without his moustache. He
stands with IRINA *and* TUZENBACH *who are on the veranda saying*
goodbye to FEDOTIK *and* RODE. *Both officers, in marching uniform,*
are going down the steps. TUZENBACH *embraces* FEDOTIK.

TUZENBACH: Dear, dear friend. Such good times we've had.
    (*Embraces* RODE.)
RODE: Once more. My dear friends, goodbye.
IRINA: *Au revoir.*
FEDOTIK: No *au revoirs*. Goodbye. We will never see each other
    again.
KULYGIN: Who can tell? (*Wipes his eyes and smiles.*) Fancy this. I'm
    beginning to cry.
IRINA: We will meet sometime.
FEDOTIK: Ten years? Fifteen? Come that time, we'll hardly
    recognize each other. We'll shake hands, and they'll be cold.
    (*Takes a photograph.*) Hold on. One more, the last time.
    (RODE *embraces* TUZENBACH.)
RODE: We will not see each other ever again.
    (*He kisses* IRINA's *hand.*)
RODE: Thank you for everything, everything.
    (FEDOTIK *is annoyed.*)
FEDOTIK: Will you hold on?
TUZENBACH: We will see each other again, God willing.
    (RODE *glances over the garden.*)

RODE: Farewell, trees.
(*He shouts 'hup-hup'.*
Silence.)
Farewell, echo.

KULYGIN: Who can tell, you might be married in Poland. Your Polish wife will snuggle up to you and call you *kochany*.
(*He laughs.*
FEDOTIK *looks at his watch.*)

FEDOTIK: Less than an hour to go. Solenyi is the only one from our battery going on the barge. The rest of us go with the line unit. Three batteries leave by batallion today, three more tomorrow. The town will have peace and quiet.

TUZENBACH: And boredom, absolute boredom.

RODE: Where is Maria Sergeeevna?

KULYGIN: Masha's in the garden.

FEDOTIK: We must say goodbye to her.

RODE: Goodbye, I must go, or I'll begin to weep . . .
(RODE *quickly embraces* TUZENBACH *and* KULYGIN *and kisses* IRINA's *hand.*)
Such splendid times we've had.
(FEDOTIK *speaks to* KULYGIN.)

FEDOTIK: A souvenir, for you, here, – a little notebook with a pencil. We can get to the river down here.
(*They both go off, glancing back.* RODE *shouts 'hup-hup'.*
KULYGIN *shouts:*)

KULYGIN: Farewell.
(RODE *and* FEDOTIK *meet* MASHA *at the back of the stage and say goodbye to her. She exits with them.*)

CHEBUTYKIN: They didn't say goodbye to me. They forgot.

IRINA: Did you?

CHEBUTYKIN: Yes. I forgot too, I suppose. Never mind, I'll see them soon, I'm going tomorrow. In one year I'll retire, I'll come back here and live my life close to you. One more year, then my pension.
(*He puts a newspaper into his pocket and takes out another.*)
Back to you I'll come and change my life. I will become so quiet, so good – good mannered, an absolute model of discretion.

58

IRINA: Do change your life, my dear. You really should.
CHEBUTYKIN: Yes. I do think so.
(*Sings quietly*) Ta-ra-ra-boom-di-ai, dance on a grave today.
KULYGIN: Beyond redemption, Ivan Romanych, beyond redemption.
CHEBUTYKIN: I could come to you for private classes. I'd be saved then.
IRINA: Fedor's shaved his moustache off. I cannot look at him.
KULYGIN: Why not?
CHEBUTYKIN: Could I tell you what your face looks like now? No, I really shouldn't.
KULYGIN: They're all doing it. It's the modus vivendi. Our headmaster shaved off his moustache, I followed suit when I became an inspector. Not one person likes it, but I do not care. I'm happy. Just as happy without a moustache as I was with. (*Sits down.*)
(ANDREI *pushes a pram with a sleeping child in it across the back of the stage.*)
IRINA: Ivan Romanych? I'm very worried. You were there on the boulevard yesterday. What happened? Tell me.
CHEBUTYKIN: What happened? Nothing. Nothing important. (*Reads the newspaper.*) It's no matter.
KULYGIN: I gather from what's being said, Solenyi and the Baron met on the boulevard outside the theatre.
TUZENBACH: Stop this. Enough.
(*He waves his hand dismissively and exits into the house.*)
KULYGIN: Outside the theatre. Solenyi started to annoy the Baron. He lost his head and said something insulting –
CHEBUTYKIN: I know nothing about it. Utter nonsense.
KULYGIN: In a seminary once some teacher wrote 'nonsensical' on an essay. The student wondered what it meant. He thought it was a Latin expression. *Non sensus.* (*Laughs.*) So, so funny. Solenyi, they say, loves Irina and he's come to hate the Baron. Understandable. A lovely girl, Irina. Like Masha a little. Lost in thought the same way. You have a sweeter nature, Irina. Masha, though, is quite sweet in her nature too. I love Masha.
(*Cries of 'A-oo' and 'hup-hup' are heard offstage at the back of*

the garden. They startle IRINA.)

IRINA: Today, everything frightens me. Why?

(Silence.)

I'm all ready as well. Tomorrow myself and the Baron marry. Tomorrow we will go down to the brickworks, the day after I will be in the schoolroom, and a new life will begin for us, please God. While I was sitting for the teacher's certificate, I broke down, it was pure joy, deep gratitude.

(Silence.)

The carrier should be coming for my things soon.

KULYGIN: All very nice indeed this, but is any of it serious? It's all very high flown, but there's precious little that is serious about it. Still I wish you well, with all my heart.

(CHEBUTYKIN *addresses* IRINA *tenderly*.)

CHEBUTYKIN: My most loved, my jewel, how far you've gone from me, I will never catch up with you. Left behind I am, an old bird, not up to migrating. I can't fly. Fly, my dears, fly and God watch over you.

(Silence.)

Shaving off your moustache was a mistake, Fedor Il'ich.

KULYGIN: Stop going on about it. *(Sighs.)* So the soldiers depart today, and life goes back to normal. Let people say what they will, Masha is a good woman, full of honour. I love her very much, I'm grateful for what I have. Fate treats people differently. Take that Kozyrio, who works in the excise here. We were at school together, and he was expelled in the fifth year because he couldn't grasp the ut-consecutive clause. These days he's poverty stricken, in the worst of health, and when I meet him, I always shout, 'Hello there, you old ut-consecutive clause'. 'Yes,' he says, 'that's it, that's it, the consecutive clause.' Then, he coughs. Now luck has always been with me. I'm happy. I even possess an Order of St Stanislav, Second Class. I myself now teach the ut-consecutive clause. Naturally, I'm clever, more clever than most, but that's no guarantee of happiness.

(*In the house the Maiden's Prayer is played on the piano.*)

IRINA: Come tomorrow, I won't hear the Maiden's Prayer again. I won't meet Protopopov again.

(*Silence.*)
As a matter of interest Protopopov is sitting in the drawing room. He's come today as well.

KULYGIN: Has the headmistress not arrived yet?

(*Strolling quietly* MASHA *crosses the back of the stage.*)

IRINA: No. They sent for her. Do you know how difficult it is for me to live alone here without Olga? She's living at the school. She's headmistress and works hard the whole day. I'm alone and I'm bored, because there is nothing to do. I've come to hate the room I live in. My decision's made. If Moscow is not to be my destiny, so be it. My fate, pure and simple. Nikolai L'vovich proposed to me. So, I turned it over in my head and the decision's made. He is a good man, so good, so very very good. I thought my soul took wings, my spirits lifted, my depression disappeared and I would work again, work. But something happened yesterday, something's hanging over me, something mysterious.

CHEBUTYKIN: Nonsense.

(NATASHA *calls through the window.*)

NATASHA: It's the headmistress.

KULYGIN: The headmistress has arrived. We'll go in.

(*He and* IRINA *exit into the house.*

CHEBUTYKIN *reads the paper and sings quietly.*)

CHEBUTYKIN: Ta-ra-ra-boom-di-ai, dance on a grave today.

(MASHA *approaches.*

ANDREI *wheels the pram at the back of the stage.*)

MASHA: Here he sits, safe and snug.

CHEBUTYKIN: So?

MASHA: Nothing.

(*She sits down. Silence.*)

MASHA: My mother, did you love her?

CHEBUTYKIN: A great deal.

MASHA: And she you?

(*There is a silence.*)

CHEBUTYKIN: I cannot remember now.

MASHA: Is the man about? Our cook, Marta, she used to call her policeman that, sometimes. The man. Is the man about?

CHEBUTYKIN: Not yet.

MASHA: A person who grabs bits of happiness, bits and pieces of it and then loses it, a person like me, slowly but surely we grow coarse, we grow angry. (*Points to her breast.*) Heat, inside, here.

(*Looks at* ANDREI *pushing the pram.*) Our brother, Andrei, look. Abandon hope. A thousand people raised a bell, the effort, the money that went into it, but down it fell without warning and broke in bits. Without warning, without sense to it. Andrei, that's his story, Andrei.

ANDREI: Will the house ever quieten down? Such a racket.

CHEBUTYKIN: Soon. (*Looks at his watch, winds it up and it chimes.*) Mine is an old-fashioned watch, it chimes. The first, second and fifth batteries will leave at one o'clock on the dot.

(*Silence.*)

I go tomorrow.

ANDREI: For ever?

CHEBUTYKIN: I don't know. In a year's time I might come back. But God alone knows. It's of no matter.

(*From far away a harp and violin play.*)

ANDREI: The town will be without life, as if someone blew it out.

(*Silence.*)

Something happened outside the theatre yesterday. Everyone is talking about it, but I know nothing of it.

CHEBUTYKIN: It's all nonsense. Solenyi began to annoy the Baron, he saw red and insulted him, and so it happened that Solenyi felt obliged to challenge him to a duel.

(CHEBUTYKIN *looks at his watch.*)

It's nearly time for it. Half-twelve, in that forest you can see across the river. Pif-paf! (*Laughs*) Solenyi likes to imagine he's Lermontov, he composes verses. A joke's one thing, but he's fighting his third duel.

MASHA: Whose third duel?

CHEBUTYKIN: Solenyi's.

MASHA: And the Baron?

CHEBUTYKIN: What about the Baron?

(*Silence.*)

MASHA: I'm completely confused. Still, I say they should not be allowed to fight. He could injure the Baron, he could even kill him.

CHEBUTYKIN: The Baron, yes, a good man, but one more or one less Baron, does it really matter? Let them fight. It's of no matter.
(*A shout of 'A-oo, hup-hup' from beyond the garden.*)
You can wait. Skvortsov, the second, he's doing the shouting. He's in the boat.
(*Silence.*)

ANDREI: If you want my opinion, to attend a duel, to be present at one, even only as a doctor, that is immoral.

CHEBUTYKIN: It only appears to be. Nothing is real in this world. We are not here, we do not exist, it only appears as if we do. And it is really of no matter.

MASHA: Talk, talk, and more talk, all the life long day. (*Moves to go.*) Living in this climate, the snow forever threatening to fall, and to top that, all this talk. (*Stops.*) I'll not go into the house, I can't bear being in there. When Vershinin arrives, tell me. (*Goes down the avenue of trees.*) The birds are leaving already. Migrants. Swans and geese. My loved ones, my lucky ones. (*Exits.*)

ANDREI: This house of ours will empty itself. The officers going, you going, my sister getting married, and me, left alone in a house.

CHEBUTYKIN: Your wife?
(FERAPONT *enters with some papers.*)

ANDREI: A wife is a wife. Mine's honest, decent, a kind heart . . . yes. But something in her hauls her down to the level of a brute beast, mean, blind, a hard hide. Not human, in some way, not her. I talk to you as my friend, the one I can lay my soul bare to. I love Natasha, that is true, but there are times when, to me, she is banal, banal, banal. I'm at a loss there, I don't know why I love her. Or rather, why did I love her?
(CHEBUTYKIN *gets up.*)

CHEBUTYKIN: Friend, I leave tomorrow, we may never see each other again. Listen to my advice. Put on your hat, grab a walking stick and walk away, walk away and keep going, and

63

don't look back. The further you go, the better.
(SOLENYI *passes across the back of the stage with two officers.*
He sees CHEBUTYKIN *and turns towards him. The officers go*
on.)

SOLENYI: It's time, doctor. Half-twelve already.
(*He greets* ANDREI.)

CHEBUTYKIN: Coming, coming. I'm tired of you all.
(*He speaks to* ANDREI.)
If I'm wanted, tell them I'm back very soon.
(*He sighs.*)
So.

SOLENYI: 'He had no time to sigh his so, the bear struck fast, he
breathed his last.'
(*Goes with* CHEBUTYKIN.)
What are you moaning about, old man?

CHEBUTYKIN: Get a move on.

SOLENYI: How do you feel?
(CHEBUTYKIN *speaks angrily.*)

CHEBUTYKIN: Out of this world.

SOLENYI: The old man worries himself for nothing. I'm not going
to overdo it. I'll leave a little wound on him, like a woodcock.
(*Takes out his scent and sprinkles it on his hands.*) I've used up a
whole bottle today, but these still stink. They smell like a
dead man's.
(*Silence.*)
Do you remember the lines 'The rebel seeks the serene
storm, believing they protect from harm'?

CHEBUTYKIN: Yes! He had no time to sigh his so, the bear struck
fast, he breathed his last.' (*Exits with* SOLENYI.
Shouts are heard.
ANDREI *enters with* FERAPONT.)

FERAPONT: Papers to sign.
(ANDREI *is edgy.*)

ANDREI: Leave me alone. Please, leave me alone. (*Exits with the*
pram.)

FERAPONT: What do I do with them if you won't sign them?
(FERAPONT *goes to the back of the stage.*
IRINA *enters with* TUZENBACH, *who wears a straw hat.*

64

KULYGIN *passes across the stage shouting for* MASHA.)

TUZENBACH: There goes the only person in this town glad to see the back of the soldiers.

IRINA: That's to be expected.

(*Silence.*)

Our town will be deserted now.

TUZENBACH: Darling, I'll be back soon.

IRINA: Where are you going?

TUZENBACH: Town, I have to go there . . . after that, see my comrades on their way.

IRINA: Not true. Nikolai, you're so worried today. Why?

(*Silence.*)

What happened yesterday outside the theatre?

(TUZENBACH *makes an impatient gesture.*)

TUZENBACH: In an hour's time I'll be back, I'll be with you again. (*Kisses her hand.*) My most loved. (*Looks searchingly into her face.*) For the past five years I've loved you and I'm still not used to it. More and more beautiful you seem to me. That hair, gorgeous, wonderful. Those eyes! Tomorrow I'll bring you away and we'll work, we'll be rich, my dreams will come true. You will be happy. Only one thing is absent, only one. You do not love me.

IRINA: I cannot do anything about that. I will be your wife, I will be loyal and obedient, but I cannot love you. What do I do? (*Weeps.*) I have never once loved in my life. Yes, I've dreamed about love. Day and night, for so long a time, I've dreamed of love, but my soul is locked, like a magnificent piano, and the key's been lost.

(*Silence.*)

You seem troubled.

TUZENBACH: All night I didn't sleep. There's nothing awful in my life, nothing to frighten me, but that lost key, it tears at my soul, it won't let me sleep. Speak to me. Anything.

(*Silence.*)

Speak to me. Anything.

IRINA: What? What? Everything is so mysterious. The old trees stand in silence.

(*She drops her head on to her breast.*)

TUZENBACH: Speak to me. Anything.

IRINA: What? What's to be said? What?

TUZENBACH: Anything.

IRINA: No more. No more.

(*Silence.*)

TUZENBACH: Small things, ludicrously small things, all of a
sudden, they come to signify your life, for no reason, none.
You laugh at them as usual, you still think of them as
nothing, but you don't have the power to prevent them.
Don't talk about it. I'm in good spirits. I think I'm seeing the
fir trees and the maples and the birch trees for the first time
in my life. They're looking at me, I think they're curious,
they're watching. Such beautiful trees, aren't they? With
them so close, life ought to be beautiful.

(*A shout is heard.*)

Time to go, I must – . Look at that tree. It's shrivelled. But
the wind moves through it like all the others. In the same
way, should I die, I will still be part of this life, come what
may. My love, goodbye. (*Kisses her hands.*) The papers you
gave me are lying on my table under the calendar.

IRINA: I'll come with you.

(TUZENBACH *is troubled.*)

TUZENBACH: Absolutely no. Irina?

IRINA: Yes?

(*He does not know what to say.*)

TUZENBACH: I've had no coffee today. Tell them to make me
some.

(*He exits quickly.*

IRINA *stands thinking, then goes to the back of the stage, sitting
down on the swing.*

ANDREI *enters with the pram.*

FERAPONT *appears.*)

FERAPONT: Andrei Sergeich, these papers are not my doing,
they're official.

ANDREI: Where is it? Where is my past? My youth, my humour,
my intelligence? I had great thoughts and big dreams. I had
hope, so much hope, for the here and now and the time to
come. We hardly begin to live, and then we grow dull,

colourless, ugly, lazy, couldn't care less, no use, no happiness – why? Our town has stood here two hundred years or more. One hundred thousand people inhabit it. And there isn't one who is not just like all the others. Not a single saint, dead or alive, not a single philosopher, not a single artist. Not a single being who is distinguished in the slightest way, who might stir up envy or desire or passion to emulate him. They eat, drink, sleep and die, that's all; more are born, to eat, drink, and sleep. And to escape the rigor mortis of boredom, they add spice to their lives with hateful gossip, vodka, gambling, and lawsuits. The wives cheat the husbands, the husbands lie, letting on they see nothing, they hear nothing. Without fail, this pile of pettiness weighs down on the children, kills the spark within them and they grow up into their fathers and their mothers – the poor, living dead.

(*Speaks angrily to* FERAPONT) What do you want?

FERAPONT: What? These papers to be signed.

ANDREI: I am weary of you.

FERAPONT: The porter inside at the Treasury Department, he was just talking. He said that this winter at Petersburg there were two hundred degrees of frost.

ANDREI: I hate the present, but that makes the future so attractive when I imagine it. Then everything will be easier, freer. I can see light far in the distance. I can see freedom. I can see my children and myself free from the laziness, the kvas, the goose and cabbage, the sleep after dinner, free from grovelling like parasites.

FERAPONT: It's said two thousand people froze to their deaths. Everybody was shaking with fear. Might have been Petersburg, might have been Moscow – I can't remember.

(ANDREI *is suddenly overcome by tenderness.*)

ANDREI: Sisters, my loved, loved sisters. (*Speaks through tears*) Masha, sister.

(NATASHA *is at the window.*)

NATASHA: Who is shouting out there? Andrei dear, is it you? You'll wake little Sophie. *Il ne faut pas faire du bruit, la Sophie est dormée déjà. Vous êtes un ours.* (*Gets angry.*) If you

67

need to talk, then give the pram and the baby to someone else.
Ferapont, take the pram away from the master.

FERAPONT: Yes, Madam.

(*He takes the pram.*

ANDREI *is embarrassed.*)

ANDREI: I'm talking quietly.

(NATASHA *pets her little boy, still at the window.*)

NATASHA: Bobik, bold Bobik, bad boy.

(ANDREI *looks through the papers.*)

ANDREI: Right you be, I'll look through these, sign what needs
signing, you can return them to the office.

(*He exits into the house, reading the papers.*

FERAPONT *pushes the pram.*

NATASHA *is at the window.*)

NATASHA: Bobik, what is Mama's name? Loved one. And who's
this? It's Auntie Olia. Say 'hello, Olia' to Auntie.

(*Two strolling musicians, an old man and a girl, enter and play on
the violin and harp.*

VERSHININ, OLGA *and* ANFISA *come out of the house and listen
in silence for a minute.*

IRINA *approaches them.*)

OLGA: Our garden is like a public road. People walk and ride right
through it. Nanny, give those musicians something.

(ANFISA *gives the musicians money.*)

ANFISA: God be with you, good souls.

(*The musicians bow and exit.*)

Poor people. You don't play for the pleasure of it.
(*Speaks to* IRINA.) Hello, my Irina. (*Kisses her.*) Child dear,
come and see the way I'm living. Come and see. In at the
school, in a flat, no rent to pay, dearest, and I'm with my loved
Olia. God's been good to me in my last days. Me, an old
sinner, and I've never lived as well in my life. The flat's big,
not a penny of rent, and I've got a whole room and a whole bed
all to myself. It's all free. I go to my sleep at night and Lord
above and his blessed Mother, there is no one happier than me
in this world.

(VERSHININ *looks at his watch.*)

VERSHININ: We'll be leaving very shortly, Olga Sergeevna. It's time.

(*Silence.*)

I wish you the very best, the very best. Where is Maria Sergeevna?

IRINA: She's about the garden. I'll go and look for her.

ANFISA: I will too. Masha, my own Masha.

(*She goes with* IRINA *into the depth of the garden.*)

VERSHININ: All things end. Here we are, parting. (*Looks at his watch.*) The town gave us some kind of lunch, we drank champagne, the mayor made a speech. I ate and I listened, but my heart was here with you all. (*Looks over the garden.*) I've grown used to you.

OLGA: Will we ever see you again?

VERSHININ: No, probably not.

(*Silence.*)

My wife and my two little girls, they're staying on here for a few months. If anything happens, or they need anything, would you –

OLGA: Yes, of course, yes. Don't worry.

(*Silence.*)

When tomorrow comes there won't be one soldier left in the town. A memory, all of it. For us, of course, a new life begins.

(*Silence.*)

Nothing happens the way we want. I didn't want to be a headmistress, but I became one. So I won't be going to Moscow.

VERSHININ: Well . . . thank you, for everything. If I did what I shouldn't, forgive me. I talked and talked and talked, forgive me for that as well. Don't think badly of me.

(OLGA *wipes her eyes.*)

OLGA: Why isn't Masha here?

VERSHININ: What more to say to you as we leave each other? What can I philosophize about? (*Laughs*) Life is hard. It seems blurred to so many of us, without hope. Still, you must concede it grows clearer, it gets more easy as time passes, and I presume, the time is not far away when it will become completely clear. (*Looks at his watch.*) Time for me to go, time. One time this species busied itself making war.

Campaigns, advances, victories, that was how we divided our time. Now, all that is out of fashion. What's left behind? A great, empty space with nothing yet to fill it up. Humankind is searching so hard for something to fill it, and we will find it sooner or later. Come that time soon.

(*Silence.*)

Yes, if we could match learning with the love of work, and the love of work with learning . . . (*Looks at his watch.*) Anyway, time I went.

OLGA: She's here.

(MASHA *enters.*

OLGA *withdraws a little to the side to let them make their farewell.*

MASHA *looks into* VERSHININ's *face.*)

VERSHININ: I've come to say goodbye to you.

MASHA: Goodbye to you.

(*There is a long kiss exchanged between them.*)

OLGA: Now, now, enough, enough.

(MASHA *weeps with violence.*)

VERSHININ: Write to me . . . Do not forget. Let me go . . . Time . . . Olga Sergeevna, here, her . . . Must go . . . Late, late, I'm . . .

(*Deeply distressed, he kisses* OLGA's *hand, embraces* MASHA *once more and exits.*)

OLGA: Now, Masha, enough. Don't, loved one.

(KULYGIN *enters in confusion.*)

KULYGIN: It's going to be all right. Weep, let her. My Masha, dear, good, my wife, you are mine and I am happy, come what may. I will not complain. You will not hear one word of blame from me. Olga, be my witness to that. We will live again as we did before, and not one word, one syllable, will you hear –

(MASHA *suppresses her sobs.*)

MASHA: I saw the shore that strides the sea,
    A green, green oak, oh green oak tree,
    A chain of gold embracing thee.
I am going mad. The shore that strides.
    A green, green oak.

OLGA: Calm, Masha, calm. Give her a drink of water.

MASHA: Not crying any more.

KULYGIN: She's stopped crying. She's very good.

(*The dull sound of a gunshot is heard from far away.*)

MASHA: I saw the shore – a green, green oak, a chain of gold, chained. Green cat. Green oak. All confused, everything. (*Drinks water.*) This foul thing, my life . . . I need nothing now, I'll be calm in a moment. It's of no matter. Why the shore? What does that mean? Why is that word stuck in my head? My brain's drowning.

(*IRINA enters.*)

OLGA: Calm, Masha. Be a good girl. We'll go inside –

(*MASHA speaks angrily.*)

MASHA: I am not going in there. (*Sobs, but stops immediately.*) I do not go into that house any more, I will not go in.

IRINA: Come on, we'll sit down for a short while, we don't need to talk. Tomorrow I'm leaving here, you know.

(*Silence.*)

KULYGIN: Yesterday I took this moustache and beard away from a boy in the third year. (*Puts on the moustache and beard.*) I look like the German teacher. (*Laughs.*) Don't I? I do. Those boys , such comedians.

MASHA: Yes, you do look like that German of yours.

(*OLGA laughs.*)

OLGA: Yes.

(*MASHA cries.*)

IRINA: Enough now, Masha.

KULYGIN: The image of him.

(*NATASHA enters, speaking to the housemaid.*)

NATASHA: What do you want? Mr Protopopov is babysitting little Sophie, and Andrei can take Bobik out for a walk. There's no end of work with children.

(*To* IRINA) Irina, tomorrow you go away, such a pity. Do stay one more week.

(*She sees* KULYGIN *and screams. He laughs, taking off the beard and moustache.*)

Get away with you, you frightened me.

(*To* IRINA) I've got used to you. You don't imagine it will be easy for me to say goodbye to you, do you? I'll move Andrei and his violin into your room. He can scrape away in there. Little Sophie we're going to install in his room. She is absolutely adorable. A little darling. This morning, she looked at me, those sweet little eyes, and she said, 'Mama'.

KULYGIN: An excellent child indeed.

NATASHA: Tomorrow, here I'll be, on my own. (*Sighs*) First things first, that avenue of fir trees is for the chop, then that maple tree. It's so terrifying and looks so ugly in the evenings.

(*To* IRINA) My dear, that belt, it does not suit you. It's dull. You need a little colour. I'll have loads of flowers planted over here, their scent – (*Harshly*) A fork, why is there a fork lying on the seat? (*Goes into the house, addressing the maid*) I am asking you why a fork is lying there on the seat? (*Shouts*) Shut your mouth.

KULYGIN: Away she goes.

(*A military march plays offstage. They all listen.*)

OLGA: They're on the march.

(CHEBUTYKIN *enters.*)

MASHA: Our men are going. So, an easy journey to them.

(*To her husband.*) We should go home. Where's my hat and coat?

KULYGIN: In the house. I took them in. I'll fetch them.

CHEBUTYKIN: Olga Sergeevna?

OLGA: Yes?

(*Silence.*)

What?

CHEBUTYKIN: Nothing. How can I tell you?

(*He whispers in her ear and alarms* OLGA.)

OLGA: This cannot be true.

CHEBUTYKIN: Yes. Bad business. I'm exhausted, worn out, I don't want to talk any more. (*Annoyed*) Anyway, it's of no matter.

MASHA: What's happened?

(OLGA *embraces* IRINA.)

OLGA: This terrible day. My dear, how can I tell you?

IRINA: What? For the love of God, tell me now. What?

72

CHEBUTYKIN: A duel. The Baron has been killed.

IRINA: I knew. I knew.

(CHEBUTYKIN *sits on a bench at the back of the stage*.)

CHEBUTYKIN: I'm worn out. (*Takes a newspaper from his pocket*.) Cry, let them cry. (*Sings quietly*) Ta-ra-ra-boom-de-ai, dance on a grave today. Does it matter really?

(*The three sisters stand, pressed close to each other*.)

MASHA: Listen, listen to the band playing. They're leaving us, the man has gone, he has gone, for ever and ever. We'll be on our own, starting our lives afresh. We have to live, we have to live.

(IRINA *puts her head on* OLGA's *breast*.)

IRINA: A time will come when we will know what this is all for. This suffering, what it is for. That which is hidden shall be revealed. Until then we have to live, we have to work, just work. Tomorrow I start out on my own, I'll teach in a school, I will give my life to whoever needs it. Yes, it's autumn, wintertime will come here soon, snow will lie everywhere, but I will work, I will work.

(OLGA *embraces both her sisters*.)

OLGA: The band plays, happily, it lifts your heart, it makes you want to live. Sweet God, time moves on. We will pass away into eternity. We will be forgotten. Our faces, voices, all of us, how many we were. Those who live after us will see our suffering turn into their joy. A happy time will come to this earth, peace. Dead generations will be remembered. With kindness, with blessing. Most loved sisters, our life is not yet finished. We are going to live. The band plays very happily, full of joy, and if we wait a little longer, I believe, we will know why we are alive, why we suffer . . . and if we knew, and if we knew . . .

(*The sound of the band gradually softens.*

KULYGIN, *happy and smiling, brings out a hat and a cloak*.

ANDREI *pushes a different pram, with Bobik sitting in it*.

CHEBUTYKIN *sings quietly*.)

CHEBUTYKIN: Ta-ra-ra-boom-de-ai, dance on a grave today. It's of no matter.

OLGA: And if we knew, and if we knew.